D0175798

Small Group Evangelism

A Training Program for Reaching Out with the Gospel

Richard Peace

INTERVARSITY PRESS
DOWNERS GROVE, ILLINOIS 60515

© 1985 by Inter-Varsity Christian Fellowship of the United States of America

An earlier version of this book was published by Zondervan Publishing House in two parts: Witness (© 1970, 1971 by Richard Peace) and A Leader's Guide to Witness (© 1971 by Richard Peace).

All rights reserved. No part of this book may be reproduced in any form without written permission from InterVarsity Press, Downers Grove, Illinois.

InterVarsity Press is the book-publishing division of Inter-Varsity Christian Fellowship, a student movement active on campus at hundreds of universities, colleges and schools of nursing. For information about local and regional activities, write IVCF, 233 Langdon St., Madison, WI 53703.

Distributed in Canada through InterVarsity Press, 860 Denison St., Unit 3, Markham, Ontario L3R 4H1, Canada.

Scripture references, unless otherwise indicated, are taken from the Holy Bible: New International Version. Copyright © 1973, 1978, by the International Bible Society. Used by permission of Zondervan Bible Publishers.

Cover photograph: Michael Goss

ISBN 0-87784-329-5

Printed in the United States of America

Library of Congress Cataloging in Publication Data
Peace, Richard.
    Small group evangelism.

    Bibliography: p.
    1. Evangelistic work.   2. Church group work.
I. Title.
BV3793.P39   1985   269'.2   85-5202
ISBN 0-87784-329-5

17   16   15   14   13   12   11   10   9   8   7   6
99   98   97   96   95   94   93   92   91   90

Dedicated in memory of my wife's parents,
Carl and Betty Boppell,
and my father, Claude Peace

Preface

Writing *Small Group Evangelism* has proved to be a more formidable project than I imagined when I started. My original intention was merely to revise *Witness* (Grand Rapids, Mich.: Zondervan, 1971) in order to bring it up to date. As it turned out, I ended up rewriting the whole book. The result is that while *Small Group Evangelism* is indebted to my original volume, it is a new book, not just a revision.

I have had a lot of help in developing *Small Group Evangelism*. A book of this kind is not written by sitting down and saying: "Now let's see . . . how can people be taught to do small group evangelism?" Rather, it is the culmination of a long process of experimentation— experimentation in how to do small group evangelism and experimentation in teaching others to do it. The experiments and insights of literally hundreds of people over the last twenty years are molded together in this volume. While it is not possible to name everyone who has contributed to this project, I do remember vividly the key experiences that helped to form these ideas.

My work in this area began while I was a member of the African Enterprise team. Our first rudimentary experiments in small group evangelism took place in Cape Town in 1967. We continued to experiment in Nairobi in 1968-69; and then in 1970 in Johannesburg we made small group evangelism the central feature of our preaching mission in that city. During the early 1970s, my wife and I ran a weekly Bible study and outreach group in our home in Newton, Massachusetts. We learned much from that group, as scores of folks, many of them from the counterculture, took part. Since moving to South Hamilton, Massachusetts, invaluable input has come from my students at Gordon-Conwell Theological Seminary, especially those who took my course entitled, "Small Group Evangelism." In particular, the class in the fall of 1982 contributed a number of insights resulting from their critique of *Witness*. They acquitted themselves admirably in that particular assignment!

Inter-Varsity Christian Fellowship chapters at universities around the country also used this material. This was largely a result of the efforts of Dietrich Gruen. I owe Dietrich a great debt of gratitude. In fact "debt of gratitude" is too mild. The continued existence of this material is, in large part, due to Dietrich. It was he who "discovered" *Witness* and promoted it in IVCF circles. He was responsible for the foundation of literally hundreds of small groups which used *Witness*. It was Dietrich who arranged to have *Witness* photocopied long after the print copies were exhausted. And it was Dietrich who urged me, constantly, to do this version. And his urging took a practical turn. He participated in the revision process itself—thinking through the nature and extent of the revising; then reacting and commenting on my new drafts. He also solicited criticisms from IVCF staff who had used *Witness*.

Other people who have contributed to the production of this volume include Jack Cook and Lyman Coleman, who have given me many insights into the process of training laypeople. My secretary Barbara DeNike patiently and skillfully translated my often illegible scrawl into a proper manuscript. And, of course, my wife Judy was present in the writing of this volume as she is in all that I write. The stimulation of her many insights and her insistence that all this must relate to "real life" have been of inestimable value.

Introduction

Since the beginning of the human race there have been small groups. It was not until the early part of this century, however, that anyone paid much attention to the special way people function in small groups. Traditionally a person had been viewed either as an isolated individual or as a member of a larger unit of society, such as an extended family or a community. But with the development of the social sciences, researchers recognized that something quite unusual and powerful happens in a small group—something which does not happen in a large group (where a different dynamic prevails) or in the casual conversation of three or four friends (when still another method of interaction takes place). In the late 1930s the scientific study of groups blossomed at Kurt Lewin's Research Center for Group Dynamics. Out of his work "group dynamics" emerged as a discipline in its own right.

The group dynamics movement has had a major impact on colleges, businesses and community groups of all sorts. Role playing, buzz sessions, T-groups, group therapy, brainstorming sessions, encounter groups and sensitivity training have become well known. Researchers have measured everything from group decision making to conflict resolution, empathetic listening to leadership styles.

The church "discovered" small groups in the 1950s and '60s. Of course, small groups had been a part of the Christian experience right from the beginning. Jesus and his twelve disciples were a small group. Benedict and then Francis of Assisi gathered their followers into small groups. Wesley's eighteenth-century revival flourished, many say, because he organized the converts into groups of ten, each with its own leaders. Still, small groups were not widespread in the church until the middle of this century. The discovery of their value seems to have been sparked by what social scientists were learning about groups. Suddenly church leaders began to speak of small groups in glowing terms: "The widespread appearance of small personal groups may be seen, in years to come, as one of the most significant religious movements of our time," wrote John Casteel in 1957.[1]

At first small groups were used mainly as "growth groups." They were intensely personal and focused on prayer, Bible study and sharing. Later the pedagogical value of small groups was recognized, and they became a part of the Sunday school and other educational aspects of the church program. Small groups were also recognized as the ideal instrument by which Christians could express their love for others through concrete acts of service.

Small Groups and Evangelism
But curiously enough, small groups were never used widely for outreach and evangelism (with a few notable exceptions, such as Inter-Varsity Christian Fellowship's evangelistic Bible studies and Campus Crusade for Christ's action groups). Their value for personal growth and renewal was recognized, but not that they may possibly be the most perfectly suited means to reach the post-Christian generation for Christ.

Although church attendance is remarkably high in America, a growing number of people have little or nothing to do with Christianity in any form. They do not attend church. It would never occur to them to do so. They do not come to Christian mass meetings. (The majority of those converted by mass evangelism appear to be nominal Christians.) They certainly do not tune into Christian television programs, except perhaps out of curiosity, much as an anthropologist might view a tribal dance. They do not read Christian books. And they often do not have any effective personal contact and dialog with individual Christians. (It is also true that a few years after conversion many Christians have lost contact with their old friends and have developed a new social network made up of Christians.) So how are we to reach these outsiders for Christ?

One powerful means may be small groups meeting in homes for serious dialog about issues of spiritual reality. Many of these people are intensely interested in spiritual things, as is evidenced by the rise of all the transpersonal psychological movements such as Scientology, est, and Arica; the Eastern religious groups like Transcendental Meditation and the Krishna Consciousness Society; and the whole New Consciousness subculture. Post-Christian Americans are very interested in spiritual reality. They just never connect this interest to Christianity or to the church. But while they will not come to church with us, they will come into our homes for a meal and for dialog.

What I am urging in this book is the deliberate use of small groups for evangelistic purposes. This may be the only way we can reach those outside the church.

One of the most appealing advantages of small groups is that they can be adapted to the needs and inclination of almost any group of people. You can reach young married couples through them, retired senior citizens, homemakers, university students, musicians, teenagers. The content, style, environment and leadership will be quite different from social group to social group—but the dynamic within the group will be the same; and so will the potential for sharing the gospel.

Small Group Evangelism has been written as a concrete guide for those who want to learn how to do evangelism through small groups. This book can be used either by an individual or a group. Once the book is read, it does not take much to start a small outreach group. Here is another appealing feature of this methodology: it does not require a lot of organization, any money or much specialized training. All you need is the willingness to invite a few friends—both Christian and non-Christian—for directed dialog around a topic through which the gospel will be seen. *Small Group Evangelism* should give you all the pointers you need to do this successfully. Of course, there is no such thing as a sure-fire, no-fail guide to evangelistic success. What this course does provide, though, is a viable way for many people to *begin* doing small group evangelism.

If you are not yet ready to invite non-Christian friends, you can use *Small Group Evangelism* with Christian friends as a personal training course in evangelism. This is the ideal way to use *Small Group Evangelism*. With people who want to learn how to share Christ and who will band together to meet for nine small group sessions of one and a half hours each, you will learn about small groups by being a small group.

The book is designed to facilitate this small group learning process. It is divided into three parts. Part 1 concerns small group dynamics, the nature of the gospel and how to use small groups in evangelism. Part 2 consists of a series of small group exercises designed to guide the group through eight training sessions in evangelism. (A ninth session is for an Outreach Event in which the group tries its hand at actually doing small group evangelism.) Part 3 contains information of use to the individual leading the small group in its training experience.

It is not hard to put together this training group on your own. You may have picked up this book out of personal curiosity. Your intention was simply to read it. What I am suggesting is that, when you have read it, you enlist six or seven Christian friends to do the first small group session together. You lead it. All the instructions you need are found in Part 3. Then decide if you want to continue. I suspect that you will want to form a training group in order to study the rest of the book together.

Small Group Evangelism can also be used as the basis of a typical thirteen-week adult education course. In this case you will have to adapt the material from a nine-week, one-and-one-half-hour time frame to a thirteen-week, one-hour-per-week experience, as I have outlined on p. 183.

Small Group Evangelism is a training course. Therefore I have included exercises to help you come to grips with the ideas in each chapter. After you have read each chapter, work through the *interaction exercises* which follow it. If you are a member of a training group, this interactive material will often be used during the small group session.

Members of training groups will also be asked to *do* something between sessions. The task will never be very time consuming nor beyond your ability. After the first session, for example, you are asked to phone one or two Christian friends and invite them to join the training group. These actions are important. So often we only read about evangelism. We never do it. By doing what is called for at the end of each small group experience, you may find yourself starting to develop an evangelistic lifestyle. It may become instinctive for you to talk about Christ with others.

Homework implies study. Study implies time. You will need time to prepare for each small group session, though not a lot of time. Fifteen minutes a day will probably suffice. Or perhaps an hour and a half on Saturday afternoon will fit better into your schedule. But *plan* your study time, especially if you have not done systematic study in recent years. And you *will* need to *study* if the course is to be of value to you. All the ideas about small group evangelism will emerge from your personal study. The small group will then serve to amplify these concepts. If you have not read the material you will not always find the small group experience of maximum value to you.

One of the most valuable experiences you will have if you go through this material with a training group is that of designing and executing what I call an "Outreach Event." This involves inviting non-Christian friends to join your group for one session during which you discuss some aspect of the Christian faith. This will be an experiment for your group through which you learn a great deal about the nuts and bolts of small group evangelism. For your friends, this will be an enjoyable evening with sincere people and interesting dialog. It may well whet their appetite for more. Pray that it will.

Beginning a Small Group Evangelism Training Program
There are a variety of ways to begin a training program in small group evangelism. Typically such a scheme is initiated by a sponsoring body of some sort—a local church, a campus fellowship, an adult Sunday-school class, the leaders of a retreat on witnessing—but this is not necessary. Whether sponsored or independent, there are certain logis-

tical details that need attention:

Group members. How do you put together a group? There are a variety of ways. Sometimes you begin with a pre-existing group. Other times, you need to recruit your own group by putting a notice in the church bulletin, personally inviting a group of people you feel might be interested or by suggesting to the appropriate church committee that this would be a good topic to study at the Adult Fellowship. Training in small group evangelism also fits nicely into the context of preparation for a large-scale evangelistic effort (a campus mission or a citywide crusade) and into the regular scheduled training of laity in the use of spiritual gifts.

It is not difficult to organize a training group on your own. When I was writing the first version of this material, a friend heard about what I was doing and asked to see a copy. I sent him the material but heard nothing further. When I saw him again six months later, he had organized a small group and had gone through the course. Through the success of the first group, others became interested. So he formed a second group and did it all over again! My friend was not particularly trained. He had a high school education, worked as an electrician, had never taught a course or led a group before and, having become a Christian as an adult, had had little exposure to Christian training.

Using this material, a retired businessman led one training group, then a second and a third. Eventually he led scores of Witness Groups (as they were then called) all over South Africa.

Do not underestimate your potential as a single individual to organize and lead a group.

Location. Where should your group meet? The first consideration is familiarity. Meet where people feel comfortable and at ease; for instance, in a home or private lounge rather than in a classroom. Then make sure the atmosphere is conducive to conversation (no intruding pets, telephones, roommates or children). It makes sense to meet near to where people live so that transportation is not a problem.

Time. You need at least one and a half hours to work through the material. Many groups find that two hours allow for a more relaxed pace. Some groups will invariably "waste" the first fifteen minutes. You may also want to plan an informal time for refreshments after the formal small group session. However you structure the time, once decided, *stick to it*. Do not consistently exceed the allotted time. Either cut down the amount of material you plan to cover or renegotiate with the group an extra fifteen or thirty minutes per week.

Invitations. Once you have decided whom you will invite and when and where you will meet, it is merely a matter of contacting people. The best invitations are person to person. Then you can convey not just the idea but your enthusiasm for it. Written invitations and telephone calls are also useful—both as the initial invitation and as follow-ups to an earlier invitation.

Size. The ideal size for a small group is between six and thirteen. Don't worry if you do not have thirteen members on the first evening, because one of the group exercises involves *inviting others* to join the group prior to week 2. If the group exceeds thirteen members, consider splitting up into smaller groups.

Delivering copies of the book. Try very hard to deliver a copy of *Small Group Evangelism* to each person *prior* to the first meeting. Have them read chapter 1 and prepare the study material. Do not apologize for this assignment. Stress that because this is a *training group*, a certain amount of preparation each week—no more than an hour or two—will be necessary. This preparation is essential for *learning*.

Another way to get people to read chapter 1 *prior* to the first session is to *add an extra session*. Make your first meeting an organizational meeting over a meal, followed by a discussion about the course. At that time you can distribute copies of the book.

Prayer. This is not simply a training course. The hope is that people's lives will be changed—the lives of Christians doing the course and the lives of non-Christians contacted. This will not happen without the work of the Holy Spirit who opens hearts and minds and moves people to new commitments. Prayer is not an option; it is crucial. As the leader you will want to pray daily for the group and its members. Also encourage the group to pray and make sure that the sponsoring body is praying.

Are you ready to begin? Read chapter 1 in preparation for your first small group session. The directions for that first small group meeting are found on p. 145. The small group leader will find useful notes beginning on p. 173.

Part 1
The
Concept

1
Understanding Outreach: The Principles of Evangelism

A church which bottlenecks its outreach by depending on its specialists—its pastors or evangelists—to do its witnessing, is living in violation of both the intention of its Head and the consistent pattern of the early Christians.
Leighton Ford

D id Jesus really expect us to fulfill the Great Commission? I mused. I had been struck once again by his all-encompassing words: "Go and make disciples of *all nations*" (Mt 28:19). On another occasion, according to Luke, Jesus told his disciples that "repentance and forgiveness of sins will be preached . . . *to all nations,* beginning at Jerusalem" (Lk 24:47). Then Luke went on (in Acts) to indicate that this ministry would take Jesus' followers from Jerusalem *"to the ends of the earth."* In the so-called longer ending of Mark's Gospel (which was probably not a part of the original document but nevertheless reflects a very early Christian understanding), Jesus says: "Go into all the world and preach the good news *to all creation*" (16:15).

The vision behind these "marching orders" was all-inclusive. Clearly Jesus meant that he had come to seek and to save all peoples.

His ministry was not simply to the Jews. His message was not simply for the first century. What he had in mind was the creation of a worldwide community bearing his name and doing his words.

But was this vision realistic? Could the *whole world* be reached? Was it possible to preach the gospel to the ends of the earth? I was baffled. How could such a gigantic task be undertaken? Even in the first century when the world was smaller and the nations fewer, it would have been an enormous job for his small band of disciples to take on the vast Roman Empire. And today it is even worse with nearly five billion people and more than two hundred countries.[1] Did our Lord give us an impossible task? Certainly this could not be the case. Surely there was a way to preach to all the nations. But *how?* That was the key question.

Equipping the Saints
In the midst of these musings, I "discovered" Ephesians 4:11-12. These two verses were the preface to a sermon I heard; but when their implications were pointed out, I quite forgot about the rest of the message because suddenly I saw how we could do what our Lord commanded. "And his [Christ's] gifts were that some should be apostles, some prophets, some evangelists, some pastors and teachers, to equip the saints for the work of ministry, for building up the body of Christ" (RSV).

What Paul is saying here is that the "work of ministry" (of which evangelism is a part) is meant to be done by "the saints," that is, by all of God's people. I had been unable to see how the whole world could be reached with the gospel because I was thinking that evangelism was done by pastors, missionaries and evangelists. (Was this a result of my experience of how churches, in fact, operate?) Of course there would never be enough evangelists or ministers to reach "all the nations." But here Paul is saying that ministry, including evangelism, is the job of laypeople! It is *our* job!

This had to be the key to world evangelization—every Christian everywhere sharing the gospel. There would never be enough evangelists to reach the world, but there are enough laypeople. By the latest count, nearly one-third of the world is Christian (at least nominally). We can, if we will, "preach the good news to all creation." What about the ministers and evangelists and missionaries? What is their job? According to Paul, their job is to train the laypeople to minister. Their role is to equip us so that we can get on effectively with the job of being God's people in the world.

Common sense supports this principle. A local church with six hundred *de facto* ministers is bound to make more of an impact than a church with only one minister plus a passive congregation. A campus Christian fellowship with thirty-five active members will make more of an impact than two hard-working officers trying to do everything by themselves. It is strange then that in today's church we seem to have developed this pattern: laypeople employ a minister to do the whole job of ministry, while others sit back as spectators—cheering the pastor on and occasionally assisting the pastor—but seldom ministering themselves, much less allowing the pastor to train them.

Leighton Ford points out that part of the blame for this misunderstanding of the nature of ministry rests with a misplaced comma! Some versions of the Bible translate Ephesians 4:12, after listing the different callings of Christian ministry, as saying, "for the equipment of the saints, for the work of ministry, for building up the body of Christ," implying there are three tasks for those called to ministry. But there should be no comma before the first two phrases! A better translation would be: "to equip God's people for work in his service" (NEB) or "His gifts were made that Christians might be properly equipped for their service" (Phillips). "The error is a small one in grammar, but a great one in practical consequences. For it now appears that the clergy's main task is not to do the work of the church, but to equip God's people to do this work."[2]

Mathematics illustrates this principle. Lest you remain skeptical of the possibility of preaching the gospel to the whole world by acting on this Pauline principle, let me share some interesting mathematics. Assume for a moment that there is only one Christian on earth. Being a faithful Christian, however, he seeks to share the gospel message with others. And in six months' time his labors are rewarded. One of his friends becomes a Christian. Together now, these two Christians carry on sharing the gospel. At the end of that first year, they each have won another to Christ. There are now four Christians.

This pattern continues through the second year. Each Christian wins one person to Christ every six months. The new converts in turn join the witnessing band. Hence in the middle of the second year, the four Christians have won four others, making a total of eight. These eight win eight others, making sixteen at the end of the second year. If this continues, at the end of the third year there will be sixty-four Christians. At the end of the fifth year there will be 1,024. Year by year the Christian community increases—more rapidly all the time. If this pattern continues unabated for just sixteen years there would be over four billion Christians—almost the present population of the whole earth! *Mathematically, in one generation, it is possible to preach the gospel to every creature!*

Now, of course, it is clear to everyone that in the nearly two thousand years we have had to preach the gospel, by no one's count could the world be considered fully Christian. Why not? What went wrong? I think it is obvious. *All too few Christians are, in fact, sharing the gospel with their friends.* Too many of us have opted out of our responsibility to be ministers for Christ's sake.

History confirms this principle. Down through the ages, whenever this principle was put into practice, spectacular results followed.

Take, for example, the New Testament church. The only way to account for the breathtaking spread of Christianity throughout the Mediterranean world is by noting the "ground-swell of spontaneous lay witness."[3] In the first century there were "no evangelizing campaigns, no mission boards and even little, if any, organized missionary activity. And yet, the Church was constantly growing."[4]

Origen, the early church historian, tells us why. "Christians do all in their power to spread the faith over the world." Christians "went on, in every place . . . sowing the saving seed of the kingdom of heaven widely throughout the whole world." And almost all of these itinerant preachers were laypeople.[5]

In the eighteenth century the great Wesleyan revival shook England. While most people recognized that this movement was sparked by John Wesley's preaching (aided by Charles Wesley's hymns), it is often forgotten that the movement grew, spread and was conserved as a direct result of the small groups which Wesley organized into witnessing bands.

In our time this principle has been vindicated in the experience of the church in South America. This church is now growing steadily as a direct result of training laypeople to be active witnesses. This effort took shape out of the frustration experienced by one of the large missionary groups, the Latin America Mission.

In the mid 1950s the Latin America Mission was worried. It had become evident to the leaders of the Mission that the church was not coping very well with the job of evangelism. In fact, it was losing ground. The growth of the population far outstripped the growth of the church. Each year, the percentage of Christians within the population decreased!

When the Latin America Mission looked at the church to see what could be done to improve matters, they were discouraged. The church seemed to be suffering from deadness and paralysis. Tired, discouraged pastors preached trite sermons to listless congregations. The only time interest could be roused was when yet another split in the church over a minor point of doctrine was imminent.

Latin America Mission was discouraged with its own attempts to rectify matters. In the years after World War 2, it had doubled its staff of missionaries. Yet this seemed to have made no appreciable impact on evangelism. Discouraging too was the fact that even though the church was not growing, other movements—mostly non-Christian— were. Determined not to give up, the leaders of Latin America Mission decided instead to take a long, hard look at these rapidly growing movements to discover and assess their secret of success.

They looked at the Communist movement. In little over one hundred years, starting from a small band of dedicated men and women, this anti-Christian movement had grown to nearly one billion people worldwide. They looked as well at the Jehovah's Witnesses.

This semi-Christian movement was growing at an annual rate of approximately four hundred per cent. They then looked at the one branch of the Christian church in South America that was actually growing—the Pentecostals. In only fifty years of work, this Christian movement had grown to fifteen million members.

What was the secret of success of these diverse movements? Certainly not a common message. What the Communist youth leader would say is almost directly opposite to the message of the Pentecostal pastor.

As Latin America Mission probed the nature of these movements, the answer emerged: Each had successfully mobilized their entire constituency in continuous outreach. Latin America Mission put their findings together in a concise statement, the so-called Strachan theorem: "The successful expansion of any movement is in direct proportion to its success in mobilising and occupying its total membership in constant propagation of its beliefs."[6]

I trust that by now this theorem sounds strangely familiar. It is really nothing more than a paraphrase of Ephesians 4:11-12. "Every layperson is meant to be active in ministry."

Lay Witness and Spiritual Gifts

But in what way are we all meant to be involved in ministry? Is it not true that certain individuals seem to have a special God-given ability to reach people with the gospel, while others fail miserably as evangelists? Here a second, complementary theological insight is vital lest we misinterpret Paul's call to lay ministry and produce an unbalanced (and hence unhealthy) Christian body. I refer to the concept of spiritual gifts.

Not only does Paul teach that every Christian is meant to be involved in active ministry; he goes further and says that the nature of this ministry involvement is defined by one's spiritual gift. In 1 Corinthians 12, he makes the following points about spiritual gifts:

1. There are different kinds of gifts (vv. 4-6).
2. Each Christian has such a gift (v. 7).
3. The Holy Spirit is the source for all the numerous gifts (vv. 8-

10); see also 12:28—13:3; Rom 12:3-8; Eph 4:11).

4. Not all have the same gift, and for the body to be healthy, it is necessary for all these different gifts to be used in concert (vv. 12-26).

These are crucial insights. The Latin America Mission failed to recognize the principle of spiritual gifts; this marred the first decade of their Evangelism-in-Depth ministry. Both in their expectation and their training, the sense was that *every* Christian was supposed to have the gift of evangelism. As a result, many Christians and churches were discouraged. In virtually every case, they failed to mobilize the whole Christian community. In more recent attempts at "total mobilization," however, the variety of spiritual gifts has been taken into account and the results have been more satisfying.[7]

What this means is that fulfilling the Great Commission requires mobilized laypeople actively using their spiritual gifts. This raises two questions: How does a person discern his or her spiritual gifts? and What role do those whose gift is *not* evangelism have in small group outreach (or in any form of evangelism, for that matter)?

Gift or Role?

The answer to the first question is beyond the scope of this book. Such discernment involves biblical study of the doctrine of spiritual gifts; experimenting with various spiritual gifts; evaluating both how you feel about the exercise of various gifts and the results you see where you use such a gift; and the confirmation by Christian brothers and sisters that indeed you have such a gift. There are a number of excellent books on this subject.[8]

Interestingly enough, small group evangelism offers to many people the ideal opportunity to test out their gifts because it requires various gifts: the gift of leadership (Rom 12:8); the gift of hospitality (1 Pet 4:9-10); the gift of encouragement (Rom 12:8); the gift of teaching (Rom 12:7); the gift of prayer (though not noted in any of the "gift-lists"—each of which are partial in any case—this gift is evident in the lives of certain Christians); and the gift of evangelism (Eph 4:11).

On discovering that there is such a thing as a gift of evangelism and, by implication, that not all have it, many Christians breathe a sigh of relief and jump to a wrong conclusion: "That is one gift I *know* I don't have, so now I can stop trying to share my faith with my friends." But this is the wrong conclusion! They are failing to distinguish between *spiritual gifts* and *Christian roles,* as Peter Wagner puts it.[9] Each Christian has a particular God-given ability (a spiritual gift) but all Christians have at least some responsibility in every area (the role of the Christian).

Wagner illustrates this with the gift of giving (Rom 12:8). He points to R. G. LeTourneau, the Texas industrialist who reverses the normal pattern of tithing. He and his wife gave away ninety per cent of their company to a Christian foundation. Of the remaining ten per cent which they kept, they gave away ninety per cent of this income! The LeTourneaus have the *gift* of giving; but it remains true that all Christians are called upon to give cheerfully to meet the needs of others (2 Cor 9:7). This is a *role* we all play.

The same distinction between gift and role applies to evangelism. Certain people have the gift of evangelism, but all Christians are called on to fulfill the role of witness. By our words and deeds it is our collective responsibility to proclaim Christ to others.

What Is a Witness?

Perhaps part of our hesitation to be faithful witnesses springs from not understanding *how* one witnesses. Hearing Tom Skinner preach or seeing Billy Graham give an invitation causes many laypeople to conclude that effective witness involves great verbal skills, even great rhetorical abilities. But in fact, a witness, according to Webster's Dictionary, is simply "a person who . . . can give a firsthand account of something." How do we give this "account of something" (actually, of *someone*)? In three ways—through our involvement, through our life and through our words. Perhaps in seeing this, our anxiety about witnessing will be quieted.

Witness through involvement. We serve as witnesses when we in-volve ourselves in one way or another in evangelistic endeavors undertaken by the church. For example, some years ago I participated in an outreach effort for youth. The churches in this particular community wanted to try to reach the real outsiders—those young people who never came near a church. They knew they could not do this by holding meetings in any church-owned buildings, so they decided to use homes for outreach. But running the project in this way meant that the help of a large number of laypeople was needed. Group leaders were required. Hosts and hostesses were needed in the homes. Christian teenagers had to provide the music. Now then, who were the witnesses in this project? Only those few people who actually spoke at the home meetings? No, everyone who participated in the project, whether by writing out invitations or by speaking, was being a witness.

We must be clear at this point because sometimes witness in such a way is disparaged. "Oh, you are just making advertising posters because you are afraid to talk about Christ to others." This may be the case. But more than once people have lost their shyness and begun to be witnesses in other more direct ways as a result of involvement in the seemingly mundane side of running an Outreach Event.

If outreach is to succeed, all the rather mechanical tasks (making posters or setting up the loudspeaker system) must be performed. But these activities ought to be only the first level of involvement in the whole work of witness. We must strive to link these activities with our witness through our life and words.

Witness through how we live. We also witness through the sort of life we live. In this sense every one of us is a witness for Christ— either good or bad—because through our actions and attitudes we say a lot about Christianity to those around us. Leighton Ford provides a good example of this:

I read recently of an American university student who tried to witness to her roommate but thought she had failed. The entire first term of her school year was a time of sickness and difficulty. To her amazement, when she came back after vacation she found that her roommate had become a Christian and gave as the reason,

"I have watched the way you have suffered."[10]
We must not pretend to be what we think a Christian ought to be, when in fact we are not that way at all. Such dishonesty puts others off because it often comes through as smug piety. What does attract— and I will say more about this later—is a real person, facing real problems, in the awesome power of Christ.

What sort of life should we then strive for? What sort of life does witness? A good, perfect life? No, we are not told in Scripture to try to be good. We are told rather "to be devoted to Christ." There is a world of difference between the two. If we are devoted to Christ, goodness will follow naturally, whereas to make goodness, not Christ, our aim is to doom ourselves to failure and probably self-righteousness as well. Peter put it well: "Simply concentrate on being completely devoted to Christ in your hearts. Be ready at any time to give a quiet and reverent answer to any man who wants a reason for the hope that you have within you" (1 Pet 3:15 Phillips).

Witness through words. This leads to the third way in which we witness—through our words. Note that Peter says that if we live a life devoted to Christ, we will, quite naturally, be questioned about this. And when we are questioned, we ought to be able to express in words "the hope" that we have. Again, Leighton Ford's experience illustrates this beautifully:

Last October we were in New Orleans. An attractive young couple asked my wife and me to lunch. As we drove along, we discovered that they were leaders in the social and business life of that city and had only been Christians a year. Two years before, they had met a captivating couple from Oklahoma City. Immediately they noticed a difference in this couple. The newcomer to town was a successful businessman, but not a slave of the business "rat race." In his wife they had observed an absence of the catty little remarks about other women, and the malicious gossip to which they were so accustomed. Finally, after a year they could stand it no longer and they asked the new couple, "Why are you so different?" And they then heard the story of how those friends had found Christ in Oklahoma City at the Billy Graham Crusade. As a result this New

Orleans couple committed their own lives to Christ.[11]
Ultimately, our aim is to be able to express in words the nature of
our faith. We must learn to do so, clearly and accurately.

We are called to be witnesses for Christ—through our involvement,
through how we live and through our words. *Our aim is to be involved
in all three ways.* And as we do so, we become what we are called
to be in this world—active witnesses for Christ's sake.

Outreach and Prayer

In addition to the concept of lay ministry and to the idea of spiritual
gifts, there is a third principle that must be discussed: the role of God
in outreach. So far the focus has been on the activity of God's people.
And this, indeed, is biblical. God in his inscrutable wisdom has
chosen to reach the world with the gospel through his people. He
could just as well have written his Word in the sky every night with
flashing lights. But he did not choose to do it that way. He chose
to work through people, so it *is* vital to explore *how* his people are
to evangelize. But it is equally vital to explore that other side of
evangelism: God's sovereign activity in opening the hearts of women
and men so that they will hear and understand the gospel. As I have
written elsewhere:

Evangelism is not all human activity. If it were, it would be
impossible. Who could change human hearts? Who is capable of
meeting profound human need? If it were all up to us, evangelism
would become manipulation. Fortunately, the other half of any
evangelistic endeavor is wrapped up in the supernatural. It is God
the Holy Spirit who both opens hearts to our message and brings
faith in Jesus Christ. It is the Holy Spirit who regenerates the lives
of those who experience conversion. Thus as evangelists we are
relieved from the burden of being successful. That is the work of
the Holy Spirit. Our call is to be faithful in doing evangelism.

So it is that prayer pervades evangelism. By prayer we recognize
our dependence on the work of God. By prayer we claim the power of God in the lives of men and women. By prayer, we receive
the guidance we need to do evangelism in God's way. So, a church

must pray from start to finish when it comes to evangelism. It has been noted that often the most successful evangelistic endeavors take place where a band of Christians have been praying for years, often with no specific project in mind, that God would reach a particular community.

Prayer is necessary for planning—that God will give us insight, guide our decisions, and empower our activities. Prayer is vital to the actual evangelizing itself—that hearts will be stirred, that Christians will be given God's message and power, and that conversions will result. Prayer is foundational to follow-up—that new believers will be stabilized, that churches will become warm, nurturing communities, and that spiritual life will prevail. In other words, you cannot evangelize unless you pray![12]

Let me summarize what I have been trying to say by putting all this in a slightly different way. Think for a moment about the world in which we live. It takes little reflection to see that it is a desperately needy place. If you doubt this—just pick up today's newspaper and circle in red all those items which deal with death, disease, international tensions, conflict or crime. You will soon find that your newspaper is a mass of red marks.

Even better, reflect for a moment on your friends, classmates, associates, relatives or neighbors. What are their problems? What tensions are they facing? Are there marriage problems? Roommate problems? Or teenagers whom parents just do not seem to understand? Is it illness? Trouble at work? The need of the world is not something "out there." It affects even those you know personally.

Turn your thoughts inward for a moment. As you do so, make a mental check list of the problems you face, the tensions with which you live, the difficult relationships with which you have to cope.

It is obvious that the world is a sad place in many ways. There is difficulty without and within. The question is, how can we cope in the face of these problems? Must we simply resign ourselves to it all and plod along as best we can, hoping for the best?

No is the ringing answer Christianity gives to the question. Life is more, far more, than dull resignation. It is true that there are many problems. But *this is why Christ came.* He came into this difficult world in which we live and lived as a man and then died and rose again from the dead—and *is still alive today.* He is alive—and calling us into a relationship with himself—a relationship of love and forgiveness, a relationship through which we are rescued from our sins and inadequacies and made—slowly but surely—into the sort of people he originally created us to be. He did not come to take us out of the world, but to be with us in the world, giving us his love and power and so enabling us to cope—to be, as Paul put it, "more than conquerors."

What an incredible message we have in the face of the needs of this world. *The world must hear this.* This is what it is waiting for.

But how will people hear this, "hear" in such a way as to grasp the significance of the message for themselves?

There is only one answer—the world must hear through us, the Christian layperson. And when we get on with the job and tell others this good news, the world will begin to change. History has shown this. If we get on with our task our city will begin to change; our friends will change; we will grow and change.

But it is up to us. God has called us to proclaim this grand message. Dare we disobey?

Interaction
Doing Evangelism: A Personal Assessment
It is one thing to *know about* the basic principles of evangelism. It is another thing to *live them out.* The purpose of the following questions is to give you a chance to reflect on where you are in relation to these three principles. Do not think of the questions as a form of judgment ("If I am a committed Christian, I'd better be living out all of this"). Rather, remembering that *each* Christian is in the process of growth, try to pinpoint where you are. In this way you will get a sense of where you need to grow.

A. Every Member a Minister
1. Do you like the idea of every Christian being called to active ministry? Why or why not?

2. What has been your past experience of ministry involvement? your present experience?

3. What have you liked most in your ministry experiences? What have you liked least? Why?

4. What has been your experience of evangelism? How do you feel about this experience?

5. How do you feel about this training course in small group evangelism? What are your hopes for it? your fears?

B. Using Spiritual Gifts

1. Read Romans 12:3-8, Ephesians 4:11-12 and 1 Corinthians 12 and make a list of the spiritual gifts named in each passage.

2. Which gift(s) do you think might be yours? On what basis do you make this judgment?

3. How can your spiritual gifts be used in the context of evangelism?

4. What is the next step for you in terms of spiritual gifts?
   □ I need to *investigate* this subject.
   □ I need to *try out* what I think might be my gift.
   □ I need to get *training* in the use of my gift.
   □ I need to start *using my gift* to reach others for Christ.
   □ I need to _____

5. What can you do, soon, to grow in this area? (For example, "I'll order a book about spiritual gifts. I'll read it daily as part of my Quiet Time. I'll pray about my gift as I seek to know what it is.")

C. Depending on God to Bring Fruit
1. What has been your experience of praying for others to find Christ? Who have you prayed for? With what result?

2. Recall experiences you have seen of God answering prayer. Recall experiences of God drawing people to himself. Recall your own experience of coming to Christ.

3. When have you prayed for God's guidance in a specific ministry activity? What has happened? How can you pray for this adventure in learning how to do small group evangelism?

2
Overcoming Doubts and Fears: The Problems in Witnessing

You have never found any problems in being a witness? You have never witnessed!

I t was the week before Christmas. I was standing alone on Boston Common. It was dark. The colored lights on all the trees were shining brightly. Snow was falling softly. Busy shoppers hurried by, laden with packages. In my hand were forty-five brochures announcing an evangelistic multimedia show to be shown that evening at a nearby church. We thought it was the perfect time to do evangelism: Christmas makes people think of the baby Jesus. They were filled with joy and love and a sense of family. They would be open to the gospel.

We were wrong, of course. Most people were filled with frustration not joy ("What can I get Aunt Mabel that she will like!"). They were thinking of how they would pay for all those presents. They certainly did not have forty-five minutes to spend watching an evangelistic show—even if it was "dazzling," "provocative" and "free" (as our brochure announced). They were in no mood to talk about Jesus.

The forty-five brochures I held were just five less than I had had one hour earlier. They did not even want our handouts! I was frustrated. I was miserable. I thought, "So this is witnessing."

I gave up and went to a show. It was dark in the cinema and I did not have to talk to a soul. So much for evangelism.

Most of us have tried to share our faith and discovered that it did not work out quite as they said it would in the "Witnessing Class." And so we ask, Why isn't our witness as easy or as successful as we were told it would be?

Part of the problem is with such courses themselves. They are often very mechanical and without much understanding of how people converse; nor do they have a very broad sense of the variety of ways in which God breaks through to people. But another part of the problem is with us. We do not like the vulnerability and the risk of rejection we are exposed to when we seek to share with another person that following Jesus Christ is the best way. And so we witness in fear, without enthusiasm, much less persistence.

A host of specific doubts and fears assail us when we think about witnessing. And it is necessary to examine these carefully lest they paralyze us even before we start. As we examine these fears, we will find that many of our fears are unfounded. What we fear will happen rarely does. And other fears, while quite real, can be overcome. This is the point of the chapter: *we do have fears and we must face them, but they can be overcome.*

If our intention to be faithful witnesses for Christ is serious, then we must confront and conquer our fear. Otherwise we will simply be play-acting, pretending to "learn how to witness," while inwardly knowing that we will probably never speak about Christ to anyone.

The first step, then, in overcoming our fear is pinpointing exactly what it is that we are worried about. The second step is admitting that we do have a problem. The third step is dealing with what we have found. We may discover that our fear is groundless and thus put it to rest by mere acquisition of accurate information. Or we may find that our fear is real and requires work on our part to overcome it. In either case, we grow in our ability to share Christ.

What follows is a list of common hindrances to witnessing, along with suggestions as to how to cope with each.

Objective Fears

There are, for example, all those fears which are quite authentic (we *cannot* do what we are being asked to do), but which can be overcome (as we learn new skills).

① *What will I say?* One such fear goes like this: "I can't share my faith because I don't know what to say. I'm a Christian and my faith is real and important, but when it comes to talking about it, my tongue gets all twisted and my thoughts never come out straight."

If this is your fear, take heart, there are a lot of Christians just like you. They find that being a Christian is one thing, talking about Christ is quite another. It is important that you listen to the inner caution you feel. If your tongue does get twisted, then you ought to spend some time and energy learning what to say. Such an investment will yield rich rewards because it is possible and relatively easy to learn how to express your faith coherently. This is the subject of chapters 6 and 7.

② *How do I say it?* A second related fear goes like this: "O.K., I understand how to express the gospel, but the fact is I never really know when it is appropriate to do so. My conversations seldom seem to get around to Christianity."

This is another problem which can be overcome. The real problem is conversational skill. Conversational ability varies from person to person. Some are naturally gregarious and friendly while others of us are shy and hesitant. But again, one can learn to be a "Christian conversationalist." This is the subject of chapter 3—learning basic conversational skills.

③ *What if I can't answer a question?* We all know this fear. There you are, in the midst of a lively conversation about Christianity. Everything has worked out. You have expressed yourself well. Your friends are interested. The context is appropriate. You seem to be getting down to the real issues. And then *the question* is asked. It is a good question. It is a *real* question. In fact, it is a question you also would like an answer to. But that is the problem. You have no answer, nothing to say. So the whole conversation stumbles to an unsatisfying and embarrassing halt. As your friends drift away, the pit of your stomach tells you you've let your side down; you're a disappointment to Jesus.

The first thing that must be said in response to this fear is that it is largely hypothetical. Such a scenario generally happens only in our imaginations. True, people do have real questions about Christianity. But these are seldom totally new or completely unexpected questions. After years of work in university evangelism, Paul Little said that he could anticipate with 95 per cent accuracy the questions that would be asked him in the course of an hour's conversation with non-Christians.[1]

So, with a little work, we can learn how to respond to most questions—not in a trivial fashion, but thoughtfully because we have begun to think through the issues. There are many good books on this subject. For example, *Know Why You Believe* by Paul E. Little (InterVarsity Press) is an overview of the twelve most common questions students ask about Christianity. John Stott's book *Basic Christianity* (IVP) and John Warwick Montgomery's *History and Christianity* (Here's Life) provide valuable data about the historical evidence for the life, death and resurrection of Jesus. Josh McDowell has written two popular books about evidences for Christianity: *Evidence That Demands a Verdict* and *More Evidence That Demands a Verdict* (Campus Crusade for Christ). Mastering even one of these books will give you great confidence in conversation as you discover that Christianity is no mere fairy tale but rests on solid historical foundations.

But what if after all this I still get asked a question I cannot answer adequately? Simply admit your ignorance! Honesty is what counts in such situations, not total knowledge. No one expects you to have an encyclopedic knowledge of Christianity. However, after saying "I don't know," take the next step and offer to hunt for an answer. Answers do exist, and the process of searching them out will be as rewarding to you as to your friend.

False Fears

While some fears are real and can be dealt with by learning a new skill or mastering new knowledge, there are other fears that are more imaginary than actual. They arise out of our feelings. And since they are irrational (in that they have little objective base), they are often difficult to deal with. These are the fears that really disrupt our witness.

What if I offend? We often suspect that our friends are not interested in Christianity and that to raise the subject will be offensive. I wonder if this fear does not have its roots in our cultural maxim that "religion and politics are not fit subjects for conversation if you want to maintain a friendship." Over and over again I have found that people really are interested in Christianity. A curious thing has happened in the United States. At the same time that fewer and fewer people know much about Christianity, there is a growing interest in the mystical and the supernatural. Along with this there is a natural and quite refreshing curiosity about Christianity. People really want to know who Jesus is and what he taught. They do not want dogma, they want data. This is not to say that, once the data is presented, there is immediate conviction that Jesus is who he claimed to be. But at least the interest is there. This is why small group evangelism is so appropriate. People want to discuss Christianity, and the small group is the ideal environment in which to do so.

What offends people is not straight talk about faith, but the pretense of being a great guru with all the answers, which we spit out in rapid-fire, pious clichés laden with a sense of judgment and an aura of superiority. This *is* offensive. Unfortunately, Christians who do this often fail to notice what they have done. Seeing that the other person is offended, they say to themselves, "The Bible tells us Christianity will be an offense to many." But it is their *manner* that offends so deeply that the listener probably could not even hear the gospel. I suspect we all know Christians like that. Such arrogance is often a cover-up for basic insecurities. In their heart of hearts they may wonder: "Is Christianity really all it is made out to be," and they cover over their doubts by trying to persuade others to accept their viewpoint. (Psychologists call this "cognitive dissonance.") What they are doing is not witnessing, but manipulating, and it is offensive.

Still, sometimes people are offended even when we are low-key, loving and sensitive. If this is the case, and Christianity is the offense, there is usually a very good reason. Probably they have had a bad experience somewhere in their past with Christians or Christianity. In this case, you will make little progress until that person is willing to talk about the bad experience. When they do open up, you may find that you have great sympathy for their feelings. Maybe a Christian friend had been a real jerk! Or you may find that what they heard (and rejected) was not really Christianity but some cultic variant which you reject too. Most people are open as long as they sense that we are being honest, sensitive and loving.

What if they reject me? Allied to the fear of offending is the fear of disapproval. Even if we are forthright about our faith, we fear we will be rejected by our family, friends or colleagues. This is a deep fear since no one likes to be rejected.

On one level, this is an authentic fear. In situations where peer pressure is strong (for example, high school, small ethnic communities), those who are "different" are excluded. While this is unpleasant (that is probably too mild a word for the excruciating pain such rejection sometimes brings), it is not your problem. It is the group's problem. If you have been loving, honest and open and this has proved to be unacceptable, you can do little more. The demand to be what you are not and to keep to yourself your deepest ideas and feelings is too high a price to pay for acceptance. So at times you may be rejected by a particular group because of your Christianity. And at times you may not have the luxury of opting out (of a family, for example). In any case, the Christian community itself often provides the fellowship which the peer group withholds.

This, however, is the worst scenario. Most groups have room for those who are "different" when they see that this difference has a positive effect. Perhaps what we really fear is disapproval and disagreement. What if we witness and our friends do not believe us? What if they think not only that we are wrong but that we are dumb?

Again, this may be more the other person's problem than your problem. One way to avoid facing an issue is to declare the issue false or spurious. But you know that Christianity is viable, both on an intellectual and an experiential level. Still, it is not easy to be laughed at. Despite the temptation to lash out, hang on to the friendship, be loving, but continue to stand for what you have discovered to be true. Recognize your need for approval but do not let it stifle your witness.

What if I fail? Some people feel that although they know they ought to share their faith, they also know that were they to attempt to do so they would botch the job. If I am going to fail, they reason, why even try?

There are several problems with this sort of reasoning. For one thing, success and failure are not the categories in which we ought to be thinking when it comes to witnessing. God does not call us to be *successful* in our witness; he calls us to be *faithful.* Results are God's concern. It is the Holy Spirit that opens hearts and minds in a way that leads to commitment. Our job is to share faithfully. Surely this is what the parable of the sower (Mk 4:1-20) teaches. Three types of *failure* are recorded before the one success is recorded. And who is it that brings about this success? Six verses later Mark tells us (in the parable of the growing seed) that it is the soil itself that produces grain, not the sower. And who prepares the soil? The Holy Spirit. Our job is to sow the seed of the Word of God. It is God who brings the increase.

Of course we can misuse this parable and the idea that faithfulness, not success, is our goal and make it an excuse for never urging commitment. But as one man put it, referring to yet another saying of Jesus, "Fishers of men are meant to *catch* men, not just to influence them. What should we think of an angler who said, 'How many fish have I caught? Oh, I haven't *caught* any, but I've *influenced* quite a few.' "[2]

There is another aspect to this fear of failure. On what basis do we assess success? Have we done our job properly only when we see people actually commit their lives to Christ? This is our heart's desire, of course, but only God knows when someone is ready to make a commitment. Perhaps the purpose of our Christian input at a particular time is simply to help someone take one more small step in the direction of Christ. You cannot measure that, but surely this movement is of kingdom value. One day that person may be helped by someone else to cross the threshold and enter the kingdom. Without your input, perhaps years before, this person might never have come to Christ.

Be faithful and let God worry about the pilgrimage of those to whom you speak.

Will I be a hypocrite? Some of us fear that if we presume to share our faith, we will lay ourselves open to the charge of hypocrisy. Who am *I* to witness? I'm not perfect. I make mistakes. There is a lot in my life about which I'm not happy or proud.

Of course all this is true. We are not perfect. No one is. This is what our theology of sin tells us. "All have sinned . . ." (Rom 3:23). The problem is not that we are imperfect but that we pretend not to be. It is pretense that lies at the root of hypocrisy—making ourselves out to be something we are not.

This is a potential problem in witness, in that a certain brand of theology says: "People will come to Christ when they see happy, successful, fulfilled people." This Jesus-makes-you-a-winner mentality confuses the end result of salvation with the process of sanctification. Salvation will one day mean that we are whole people standing before a holy Lord. But at the moment we are weak people who are slowly being made whole by a powerful Lord.

So the issue in witness is not how do I become good enough to share Christ. Rather it is how do I learn to be honest enough to share how Christ enables me to cope with my weakness. What intrigues non-Christians is the discovery of an imperfect person (as they are) with real problems (like theirs), coping with these in the awesome power of Christ. The question is not, Are we perfect? but, Are we growing? As John White has stated: "Don't wait to witness until you are perfect. Witnessing involves being honest all the time—now. Never cover up your weaknesses in order to witness. What the world is waiting to see is not a perfect Christian, but the miracle of grace working in a weak, imperfect Christian."[3]

What if I'm not growing as a Christian? It is all well and good to say that continuing growth, not perfection, is the important thing. But what if you are not growing? What if Christ seems distant to you? What if the faith-realities you affirm seem little more than lifeless mental propositions? Surely this affects your ability to witness.

Again, this is not an unusual experience. In the course of a lifetime, all Christians go through cycles of dryness during which their faith seems unreal. Sometimes we can point to a reason for this sense of alienation. Perhaps, for example, we are simply not giving ourselves to the spiritual disciplines that produce a vital spiritual life. We do not pray. We seldom read Scripture. We have little fellowship. We seldom attend church. No wonder Christ seems distant. He *is* in that we simply are not opening ourselves to his presence. (He is always there, but we are not always aware of him.) We probably will not have much motivation to witness. At such times we need to reopen our lives to Christ. This often involves building into our busy lifestyle regular, quality time with Christ and his people. It will not be easy, but it is crucial.

At other times, we may go through a spiritual dry period without knowing why. We pray but the words echo off the ceiling. We study the Bible, but it is without life. We worship, but our mind wanders into trivia. An abundant body of literature from all ages indicates that such dryness is quite normal. It will pass. And in retrospect you will see that you learned valuable lessons that would otherwise not have been possible. Such a "dark night of the soul" is not comfortable but it is of value as we persevere.

But how do we witness when Christ seems distant? Just as we witness at any other time. We reflect honestly what we know of Christ and do not pretend to be what we are not. Witnessing is harder during such periods but potentially quite fruitful since we do not come at people with too many answers and too much confidence. And so the power of weakness (which is the power of God) breaks through to others.

Is Christ really the only way? We will not witness if we do not feel we have something true, vital and powerful to say. Why bother? Especially since we live in an age that tells us that all truth is equal and that truth in an absolute form probably does not exist. This spirit of the age affects us on a very deep level. It makes us wary of intruding on anyone else's ideological or experiential "turf." "Who am I," we reason, "to claim that Christ is *the* Way, *the* Truth and *the* Life?" That seems both assertive and narrow. And so we are silent.

If this finds an echo in your mind, remember this: *you* did not make up the idea that Jesus is the only way. This is Jesus' own assertion. You are merely quoting him (Jn 14:6).

Of course, this raises the related question: Who is Jesus to assert such things? If he is, indeed, the incarnate God, diety come in human flesh, then for him to make such a statement makes perfect sense. In fact, *not* to have said it would have been deceitful. Worse, by withholding the only truth able to save people, he would have become a despiser of people. But he did not do that. Jesus said quite plainly, "I am the Way, the Truth and the Life." He said this because that is precisely who he is.

The second issue we must grapple with is the deep and insidious impact of our culture on our attitudes. Twentieth-century culture does not like absolute statements. It is very hard for most of us to say, "Jesus is the Way," lest our friends misunderstand us, or hear this as a word of judgment, or feel we are arrogant.

And, of course, we do not want to be arrogant. What we need is the attitude which D. T. Niles commends when he says that evangelism is "one beggar telling another beggar where to find Bread."[4] The correct attitude by which to assert truth statements is that of the beggar—humble, without pretense, aware that in ourselves there is little to commend us. Niles's comment also makes it clear that we need to have real Bread to offer. Otherwise, we raise false hope and ultimately do others a grave disservice. It is not by chance that Jesus also asserts "I am the bread of Life" (Jn 6:35).

What if I'm not a Christian? This seems a strange concern. Why would this question be raised by anyone reading this sort of book?

Because learning to share Christ raises the whole question of our own relationship with Christ. People come into contact with Christ in such a variety of ways. For some, it is vividly clear when they met Christ; they can point to a particular time and place. But for others, say, those who grew up in a church, the answer to the question "Do I know Christ?" is not quite so obvious. They attend church. They believe in Christian ideas and values. They are active in service. Still they ask themselves: "Why am I involved in Christianity? Is it just because my parents were Christians and took me to church? Am I here simply because I cherish the quality of the friendships or the good music or the values? On a deep level, do I live in relationship to Christ?" Without the certainty of a dramatic adult conversion experience, these are not untypical questions.

Nor are they inappropriate questions. We all have to face this issue squarely: Do I know Christ? Have I opened my life to Christ in repentance and faith? At the core of my life, is Jesus the Lord and Master whom I actively follow?

Is Jesus your Lord? Until you settle this question, your witness will, of necessity, be tentative. You cannot really speak to others about Christianity in any power or depth until you have come to grips with and resolved this issue for yourself. You cannot talk about Christ until you have met him.

All this gives us a valuable clue to the essence of witness itself. We focus in conversation not on an ethic, an organization, an ideology, a lifestyle, or even a set of doctrines. We may touch on these aspects because each is a part of the total Christian world view. But at the heart of the gospel is a *relationship* between a living person and the living Christ. Jesus is the focus of our witness. To attempt to make any of these other aspects fundamental is to rob Christianity of its essence.

Neither do we witness to one particular way of coming into relationship with Christ. Some people come to Christ suddenly, some slowly. For some it involves a gradual turn, spanning many years. For others the turning takes place in stages, with a series of discernible events marking their pathway. Still others (like Paul) are converted in a flash with no discernible preparation. How we meet Christ is not the issue. The issue is whether we have come to him in repentance and faith and know it.

A Sense of Insufficiency
While various fears may be the major impediment to active witnessing, a sense of insufficiency will also hinder how we share our faith. This is the feeling that we lack something crucial to do the job. For example, we say, "I would witness, if only I had the time, or if I had the motivation, or if I had the faith." We feel that if we could gain these elusive elements—time, motivation, faith—then we would witness.

Insufficient time. We all consider ourselves to be busy people. And we are. Our days are full—and we do not see how we can take on another thing. And yet, *we are able to meet unexpected demands on our time.* For example, a friend phones and says he has tickets for Saturday's football game. We need no persuading to accompany him. And yet, on Saturday we had planned to start painting the spare bedroom. But it can wait. . . . And so it goes. When we think about it, it really is not a question of "no available time," is it? It is basically a question of priorities. *We do what we want to do.* We are able to make time for whatever grips us.

It would be interesting (though disconcerting) to keep track of how we spend our time during an average week. One friend who did this was horrified to discover how much time he spent at sports. Another discovered that he averaged two hours a day gardening.

Now neither gardening nor sports is wrong, but the question remains: Is the amount of time we spend on these activities out of proportion to the time we devote to what we *say* is most important to us?

Insufficient motivation. The problem of time is really a problem of motivation. If we are motivated, we will find the time to do quite a lot. But so often we are not motivated as Christians to share our faith with others. Why is this? We have a message which this world desperately needs. And yet when one compares the motivation level of the average Christian to the motivation level of the average cult member the comparison is devastating.

What ought to motivate us to witness? One thing, of course, is our Lord's command: "Go and make disciples of all nations." As our Lord, he has the right to command our obedience. Still, this is an external motivation—someone telling us to do something. It is a legitimate motivation, but it is a commandment which comes from outside ourselves.

A deeper and more powerful motivation is that which arises out of the richness of our personal experience of Christ. "I know Christ's love and hence I cannot help but tell others." If we do not feel motivated to share Christ, perhaps it is because we have not nurtured our own relationship with him. *At the root of the loss of motivation is the loss of experience.* The answer to this very real problem may be found in the small group experience itself. When we seem to be struggling spiritually, it is often through our brothers and sisters in Christ in the context of a fellowship group that we begin to recover our sense of God's presence.

Insufficient faith. I do not think we have yet got to the root of the motivation problem. Quite frankly, for me, the problem of motivation was really a problem of faith. When I was younger, what most deeply hindered my witness was the uncertainty I felt as to whether Christ was indeed the answer to everyone's need. He was the answer to my needs. I believed this. I experienced this. Yet when I was honest, I knew that there was a core of uncertainty within me when it came to others. I was not sure they also needed him.

I could look at the confident young man with the expensive suit, beautiful girlfriend, sports car and excellent job. Here is a man who has no needs at all, I thought. He has it made. He probably does not need Christ.

I only began to cope with this problem of unbelief when I started to see beneath surface appearances. It was a major revelation for me to discover that everyone wears a mask over his or her true self, revealing only a carefully chosen image in public. But beneath the mask, at the point of our real self, deep needs reside—inner loneliness, quiet desperation, lack of motivation, fears, guilt, uncertainty. *And we are all like this.* No one is exempt. We all need Christ. Any effort at witness will be half-hearted until we know that other people do need Christ.

How does one cope with this sense of unbelief? I can give no easy answer, except to say that you must investigate this issue on several levels. For one thing, you must ask yourself the key question: Do I really believe that Christ is the unique Son of God, the one whose life, death and resurrection opened up for people the possibility of knowing God? You must allow your *mind* to be persuaded that Christianity is true and that Christ is who he claimed to be.

But once your mind is convinced, then your emotions must also be persuaded. You must *know* within yourself the reality of human need for God. This is an awareness which grows as we grow in Christ. It is an awareness which, in some senses, only God himself can give us. If this is your problem, perhaps you ought to pray for the vision to see people as they really are.

Misunderstanding Evangelism

For some, it is not fear and it is not a feeling of lack which hinders us in our witness. Rather, it is a misunderstanding of what evangelism and witness are all about.

A lot of sincere Christians are highly dubious about the value of evangelism. The reason for this is that to them evangelism is associated with emotionalism, exploitation of people, tearful confessions, hypocrisy and high-pressure manipulation. Their image of an evangelistic meeting is a cross between a high-powered political rally and the circus. No wonder that for some *evangelism* has almost become a theological swear word.

Unfortunately, these images have some basis in fact. Many abuses have been perpetrated in the name of evangelism. But such offensive activities are not an inherent part of evangelism. They are distortions, not distinctives, of evangelism. The essence of evangelism is not a peculiar *method,* but a particular *message*—a message about Christ's life, death and resurrection. The forms and methods through which this message is presented can vary widely. So do not be put off by evangelism because in your mind it is associated with methods with which you cannot identify.

Others are suspicious of evangelism because they feel that it is irrelevant to what they understand to be the "real issues" in the world today—such as hunger, racial hatred and war. Once again, I must say that in some instances this charge is accurate. Some Christians have felt that their duty to the world was fulfilled by sitting in a seat at an evangelistic rally. Concerned about their neighbors' spiritual needs, they forgot about their physical needs.

But this is not the biblical pattern. James has stern words for such people: "If a fellow man or woman has no clothes to wear and nothing to eat, and one of you say, 'Good luck to you, I hope you'll keep warm and find enough to eat,' and yet give them nothing to meet their physical needs, what on earth is the good of that?" (2:15-16 Phillips).

Our Lord combined in his own ministry a concern for the physical with a concern for the spiritual. He saw people as whole beings, with both physical and spiritual needs. To avoid meeting either need is to be unfaithful to the wholeness of the gospel. True evangelism must reflect this.

Both emphases are needed. It has often been said that the reason there are so many social problems is that "not enough people care." True enough. But often people do not care because they cannot care. Their own problems are so deep and so consuming that they can only be concerned about themselves. Such people can begin to care only when they start to cope with these personal needs. This becomes possible when they find new life in Christ. Evangelism is therefore the foundation for social concern, in that by finding Christ, individuals are freed enough from their own needs to be able to reach out to meet the needs of others. The dichotomy between evangelism and social concern is a false one.

If you are hindered in your witness because you believe evangelism involves certain "techniques," rest assured that this is not so. The deepest and finest witness occurs when we are the most transparently open to others—allowing them to see and to hear Christ through us.

Our problem is that most of us go to great lengths to avoid even mentioning Christ!

Interaction

Witnessing and Me

Few of us are consistent verbal witnesses for Christ because we are hindered in one way or another. As we strive to become witnesses, we must come to the point where we face up to our particular hindrances, and then decide how to cope with them.

Read through the following questions slowly and meditatively to see which ones most accurately reflect where you are at right now. Check those answers which you feel describe your own feelings or usual reactions to "evangelism," even if they may not be the ideal reactions and feelings you hope to have some day.

1. I experience some difficulty in talking about Christ with others   _____
because:

    a. I am afraid I will offend if I do.   _____

    b. I really don't know what I would say if I tried to talk to another-   _____
er person.

    c. I do not feel my gift is talking about Christ with others.   _____

    d. If I did get into a discussion I just know I would be unable to   _____
answer questions which might be asked.

    e. I guess, when you get right down to it, I'm not terribly sure   _____
my friends need Christ.

    f. I have seen Christians "witnessing" to others, and I would be   _____
terribly embarrassed to do that sort of thing.

    g. I'm afraid I'm not sure whether I could say I have any sort of   _____
vital relationship with Christ.

    h. Though I do know Christ, I fear I seldom experience his pow-   _____
er and influence in my life.

    i. I am afraid others won't accept what I say.   _____

    j. I don't want to be a hypocrite.   _____

    k. I am just not motivated to witness.   _____

    l. I believe evangelism is really for the cults.   _____

    m. I just don't like to intrude my views on others.   _____

    n. I am really not very good at conversation, especially those   _____
that are heavy.

    o. My real fear is that if I talk about my faith, my friends might   _____
reject me.

    p. I know that if I try, I won't do a good job; so why try because   _____

who likes to fail?
q. I don't have any significant friendships with non-Christians. _____
r. Who am I to talk? My life is not so great. _____
s. I really don't have the time to get involved with others in this _____
way.
t. I guess that I am not so sure that Christ is the only way to _____
God.
u. My friends are really not interested in Christianity. _____
v. If I do evangelism I won't have time to care for the needy peo- _____
ple that Christ calls me to.

2. Go back over each of the ones you checked. Next to each, indicate whether they can be dealt with by training, study or practice. Which are the most pressing problems? List below how you might begin to cope with the key problems.

3. In the days to come, be particularly sensitive to natural opportunities which arise in which you can speak about Christ. List the people for whom such opportunities will probably come up.

4. I am reticent to get involved in any organized evangelistic effort because:
a. I don't have the time. (As you evaluate how you use your time, determine how you could change your timetable to get more involved in evangelistic activities.)

b. I just don't like "evangelism" and am hesitant to be associated with such endeavors. What I dislike about evangelism is

A Covenant with God

To undertake this training program is an act of faith and an act of commitment. Read through the following covenant statement. I hope that after prayerful consideration you will be able to commit yourself to God in this way.

"Having thought through my own feelings, I am willing to undertake this training course as an act of faith. Hence I commit myself before God to:

1. Give this course *top priority* for the next nine weeks, by attending faithfully, reading and studying diligently, and acting consistently to put into practice what I learn;

2. Open myself to the *influence of the Holy Spirit,* to learn from him;

3. Open myself to the *power and presence of Christ* so as to come to know him in a deeper, richer way;

4. Open myself to *my friends,* so as to share with them what I am learning of Christ;

5. Open myself to the *others in the group,* so as to learn from them and to share with them what I know from my own unique, God-given perspective."

If you are able freely to commit yourself in such a way, you will find your response of faith answered in ways you cannot begin to anticipate. May God give you the faith to do so.

Lord, you know me so well. You know all the excuses I use to avoid talking about you with others. I present these excuses to you now. Help me to become free and natural as I talk about you. May I know your power in my life so that when I speak it will be out of a vital relationship with you. Lord, as your very weak and inadequate servant, I now offer to you what talents I have. Use them far beyond my expectation. Make my experience of sharing you with others a joyous one. Amen.

3
Communicating Our Faith: The Skills of a Christian Conversationalist

Our task as laymen is to live our personal communion with Christ with such intensity as to make it contagious.
Paul Tournier

I t ought to be easy to talk about our faith with others. After all, if Christian commitment is the core of our life, then it should be difficult to avoid mentioning Christ in the course of ordinary conversation.

But this is not how it works. Most of us simply do not talk about the difference faith makes to how we live; or how our relationship with Christ has given us new meaning in life; or how we came to the conviction that Christ is the unique Son of God. Why not? Why isn't conversation about Christ simple and natural?

For one thing we are inhibited by our culture. In most circumstances, faith is not a topic of conversation. It does not come up naturally in the cafeteria line or at parties. We may talk informally about sex, money and drugs, but talk about Christ is unusual (even though most people are very interested in him). So since faith is not on our cultural agenda, it takes effort to bring it up.

Part of the problem is personal, however, not cultural. When we try to talk about Christianity, we find we don't have the right words to convey faith concepts. If we mention repentance or salvation, much less justification or redemption, our friends simply stare at us. They do not know what we mean.

But our failure to be honest is probably the greatest hindrance to easy and natural conversational witness. Except with Christian friends, we are uncomfortable discussing faith. We have not learned to be honest.

Witnessing does not mean learning new "techniques," or repeating a rote pattern of words, but simply being honest. Witnessing, according to John White, is

> being true to what God has made you in your speech and in your day-by-day behavior. Such honesty will demand that you talk about Christ to unbelievers with whom you converse. The fact that you have in the past had to create openings to talk about spiritual things proves that subconsciously you have been avoiding the openings that are continually being presented to you. . . . If you are even partially honest (total honesty is rare and difficult) in a conversation with an unbeliever, you will find it extremely difficult to avoid talking about Christian things. Do you say it is difficult to witness? I maintain that with a little honesty, it is almost impossible not to witness.[1]

Once, when I spoke to a Bible study group about this, a woman came up to me and said: "I think I know what you mean. This evening, as I was leaving for this Bible study, my neighbor asked me where I was going. I said, 'Oh, I'm going to a friend's house.' Now this was true, but I have a feeling that we would have got into a really interesting conversation if I had been fully honest and said, 'Oh, to a friend's house *where we have a weekly Bible study.*' But I didn't do this because I was afraid he might want to talk about the Bible study."

Her experience is typical. Instead of being open about our faith in Christ, many of us actually avoid opportunities to talk about him! We ought to aim to become what Bruce Larson calls a "Christian conversationalist":

To have dialogue with a gifted Christian conversationalist is a rare and wonderful experience. I will always be thankful for a conversation I had with such a person. He listened to me. He was interested in my struggles, doubts, and hopes. He seemed to understand me. He shared some of the concerns of his own life which were very much like my own. From time to time he asked questions. Finally he prayed with me, not in a condescending way but as a fellow seeker trying to discover God's best. I came away from that conversation a different person. . . . People are eager for love and acceptance. Through the art of conversation we can demonstrate that God knows them, loves them, and understands them.[2]
But how do we become "Christian conversationalists"?

Honesty
Honesty is the first step, but honesty is not easy. We all like to put our best foot forward, to have people like us; and we all secretly fear that if people really knew us they would not like us. Early in life we learn to wear disguises and so appear to be what we think pleases others. And this lack of transparency carries over into our witnessing. Our habitual instinct is to disguise our faith.

But honesty can be learned. Begin by being honest with yourself. Then be honest with those people closest to you. Then widen this circle of honesty to include families, friends, acquaintances and, finally, strangers. *Our aim is to make openness a reflex.*[3]

Be aware that the degree of honesty must be appropriate to the particular relationship. What you share with your husband or wife, for example, is not necessarily appropriate to share with your neighbor. Sometimes when people discover the idea of honesty, they feel they must run out and tell all to everybody. Not only might this be embarrassing to the hearer ("Why is he telling me this? This has nothing to do with me."), but such revelations may harm other people in your life. The aim is to develop a transparent personality—not to share your whole life indiscriminately.

Also, honesty involves sharing dreams as well as failures: What do we aspire to? When have we felt really loved? What moves us?

Finally, though honesty is our goal, no one can be completely transparent. We will grow in our ability to be transparent as we aim to be people whom others describe as without guile or deceit.

Communication Skills

But honesty alone is not enough. It supplies the intention and will, but we may still be handicapped by our relative lack of communication *skills*. Communication is a funny thing. We do it all the time. We could not function in society were we not able to communicate. As a result, we come to feel that communication is easy and natural, like eating and sleeping. And so it never occurs to us that we need to learn anything more about communication.

The problem in communication is *noise*. Noise has become a technical term used by communication theorists to describe "anything that disrupts, distorts or distracts our messages." Sometimes this is physical noise. Your apartment, for example, may be near a busy freeway, making it impossible to hold a dinner party. The guests cannot hear each other over the din of the traffic. Or it may be psychological noise. The inner environment of the listener disrupts the message. You are telling a friend about your great date last night, but he is thinking about the test he is about to fail during the next class.

The aim in all communication is to overcome noise and thus convey what is in our heads to the heads of our listeners with minimal distortion. How can we do this? What are the conversational skills that promote clear communication?

Speaking with clarity. Some people assume that everyone thinks as they think. With little regard to careful word choice, grammar or syntax, they simply spew out ideas in stream of consciousness fashion. But everyone does not think alike. Each person interprets the world through an internal grid, and no two grids are alike. Everyone knows what the noun *cat* refers to, and can distinguish it from a dog or a banana. But *cat* may *feel* quite differently to each person. One person may have grown up with cats and love nothing better than sitting in front of a fire with a good book and a purring cat. Another person may have been bitten by a wild farm cat as a child and has hated cats ever since. Still another is allergic to them. So the word *cat* evokes something different for each of these people.

Some words generate a particularly strong reaction, far beyond what their definition alone can explain. In the 1950s the word *Communist* created a hysterical reaction in many Americans. In the 1960s the word *hippy* provoked the ire of many. In the 1970s the word *Vietnam* generated enormous feeling. In the 1980s words like *abortion* and *nuclear freeze* arouse strong emotion.

Words possess not only content but a feeling-tone. Christians feel good about the word *repentance,* understanding that repentance brings great hope: we can change and be forgiven. But for our non-Christian friends, this word reeks of sawdust trails and weeping penitents—it has no possible relevance to them!

We must also pay attention to the *content* of the words we use. What good is there in using a theological term which we understand if our unchurched friends do not? Even if it has no negative feel, it is not useful if they fail to grasp its meaning. We must talk about repentance, but we must do so in words and phrases which are understood. Instead of using the word *repentance,* we can point out that everybody's life is going in one of two directions: either toward God (and hence toward life and wholeness), or away from God (toward death and disintegration). If we are going away from God, we need to stop and decide to turn around and follow God's ways. That is the essence of repentance. You can talk about it without using a single theological word except *God.* (For some people you may even need to explain *God.*)

Learning to talk about the gospel without theological terminology is not an optional skill. To use theological words without translation will mean that many will *misunderstand* the gospel. They simply cannot understand what we are saying, and so they will come to erroneous conclusions about the gospel.

It takes effort and skill, therefore, to convey both the objective content and subjective feeling of your ideas. Fortunately, conversation allows ample opportunity for feedback which is the best cure for noise. *Feedback* simply refers to the give and take of questions and answers in ordinary conversation.

Your cat-hating friend, for example, asserts: "It's obvious that you actually like cats. I find that quite disgusting and hard to understand. They are such vicious creatures!"

"Cats vicious? I've never met a vicious cat," you reply. "Let me tell you about Ginger. If ever there was a loving cat—" and you launch into a warm, cuddly cat story.

Your friend responds with her story of getting bitten. And slowly, by dialog, each begins to understand how and why the other feels as they do about cats.

This is feedback. It is essential to clarity in conversation. This is why witnessing as monolog is almost always a failure. Simply to dump a bunch of theological phrases in rapid fashion onto an unsuspecting stranger in a shopping mall is not witness. Instead, you must create the kind of situation that allows for feedback, where give and take is possible until clarity is achieved. (This, by the way, is what a small group provides.)

There are at least two other ways to improve the chances that your message will be understood: the use of creative redundancy and the use of multiple communication channels. In communication, *redundancy* is simply repetition to ensure full transmission. The more the message is heard the better the chances that it will be understood. *Creative* redundancy means repeating the same message in a variety of ways. Simple repetition of the same words will quickly be tuned out, whereas communicating the core message in a different fashion each time greatly helps a person grasp what you are saying. Using *multiple channels* achieves the same end. Instead of just saying it over a telephone, say it in person, where your body language complements your message. In addition, bring along a one page handout of your message. Three message channels (voice, body, print) are better than one (voice only).

Listening with care. Listening is another skill crucial to effective communication and effective witness. When we listen carefully, we hear what interests other people (and so learn how to capture their attention). We come to understand the words and images that make up their inner grid, or world view, and we thereby enhance our ability to communicate effectively. We hear of the needs and aspirations of other people and thus learn where Christ can touch them.

Of course, good communication involves not only us but other people. The more carefully *they* listen, the better the chances they will understand. But this is the rub. How can we get people to listen carefully?

Others will listen to us when they see that we are listening to them. If we have not listened, how can we expect them to accord us the same courtesy? We often gain the right to speak at all only after having listened to their concerns. When we have heard their story, they may want to hear ours.

Sometimes listening alone is enough. One morning while a minister was preparing his Sunday sermon, he was interrupted by a telephone call. A distraught parishioner asked if she could come over immediately to discuss a terrible problem. He agreed and soon she arrived. She began talking as she sat down, and for the next forty minutes poured out her heart. All the minister did was nod at appropriate moments to indicate he understood. Suddenly she finished. She smiled and was relaxed as she got up. Then she thanked the minister profusely for all the help he had given her and left, a changed woman. He had merely listened while she sorted out her own problem!

There is yet another side to this whole problem. *People will listen to us when we capture their attention.* It is that simple—and that difficult. For there is a lot of competition out there for people's attention. Radios blare catchy music. Billboards flash provocative images. Television seduces with its simplistic view of reality. Headlines and easy-to-read articles in newspapers demand that we read them. We are bombarded with so many voices that we screen out most of them without much thought. So we must ask: What will prevent that other person from tuning out *my* message?

We may capture people's attention in a variety of ways. Our friends listen to us simply because they are our friends and we are important to them. (Which is a strong clue as to whom we ought to be sharing our faith with!) Or we capture attention by telling a funny story or an anecdote. Perhaps we use vivid words or arresting metaphors. But most important, people will listen to us when they sense that we have something to say that is important to them. They will listen when we are touching on real needs or aspirations in their lives.

This is crucial. We need to develop a sensitivity to the needs and aspirations of others. True, Christ came to deal with our sin. But different people experience sin in different ways. For some people, it is the trail of wrecked relationships that finally jars them into realizing they have a problem. For others, personal need is recognized through loneliness, lack of purpose, or deep anxiety. Still others fear death or find themselves crippled by a destructive dependency—to drugs, alcohol, sex, money, food or TV. In each case Christ can deal with their particular problem. And they will listen to us if we address them on this level. It is one thing to say "Christ died for your sin." It is quite another to say to a friend who feels no purpose in life: "Jesus wants you to take part in the building of his kingdom. There is much need out there—hungry people, hurting families, evil structures. When you come to Jesus, you will have so much purpose for living, you won't have time to sleep, if you're not careful!"

But how do we know the need in another person's life? By being in an honest, loving relationship with that person. Most people find it hard to admit need. But if we have been open and honest, and they have watched us own and cope with our need, they too will be open. Then we can share how Christ can meet their need.

A Christian conversationalist, therefore, is one who is open and honest, listens intently, and speaks with care and clarity to the real needs in another's life. This is not a skill easily or quickly learned, but it can be mastered. So, each of us must work on conversational abilities, for the sake of the kingdom.

Interaction

Sharing Our Faith with Others

"Me talk about Christianity? I wish I could but I just can't! What would I say?"

How often have *you* felt like this? You are not alone in your feeling. Most people avoid sharing their faith with the same fervor that they would avoid sharing the plague. It is strange, is it not, how hard it seems to be to talk about Christ with nonchurch friends?

Yet, sharing with others the exciting things Christ has done is the norm in the New Testament. Perhaps there are some lessons here for us in Mark 5:1-20. Read the passage and answer the following questions about the story in Mark 5:

1. *Who* are mentioned in this story?

2. This story took place at the side of a lake "where there were many caves in the limestone rock, and many of these caves were used as tombs in which bodies were laid. At the best of times, it was an eerie place; as night fell it must have been grim indeed."[4] Using the text and a Bible map, try to locate the area.

3. What title did the man use to address Jesus?

Though men often hesitate in their judgment of who Jesus is, note that the supernatural beings knew exactly who he was.

4. From what you know of Jewish dietary laws, could these herdsmen have been Jews? Why or why not?

5. Imagine now that you are a journalist. Here is a good story for you. Write an account of this incident in your own words as if you were doing so for the *Palestine Times*. Include: (a) a vivid description of the man and his history; (b) his encounter with Jesus; (c) the reaction of the demons, and their end; and (d) the response of the local population.

6. What was the first reaction of the populace to Jesus? Why do you suppose they reacted to him as they did?

7. What was their second reaction to him, after he had left?

8. What changed their minds?

9. What does this teach you about the value of sharing with your neighbors what Jesus has done?

10. What do you suppose the cured demoniac told his friends about Jesus?

11. What could you tell your friends that Jesus has done for you? Be honest and be natural in answering. Spend time on this, and then share it with someone.

Every venture has a beginning. So too with sharing our faith. Our initial attempts may well sound unnatural and strained, but they are beginnings and quite necessary. *Today* is the day to start sharing, not tomorrow. Try to be conscious today of wanting to share your faith. Sharing the truth of Christ with a friend is an act of love. This is part of what it means to love others.[5]

Prayer and Witness
One of the first steps in becoming a witness is thinking about the people with whom we have natural contact. So this week:
1. *Make a list* of the people with whom you could share your faith. Think about your neighbors, friends, classmates, colleagues, relatives and so on. Do this prayerfully. Let God direct your thinking.

2. *Pray* for these people. Pray for their needs. Pray that you will have the chance to speak to at least one of these people this week about Christianity.
3. *Be sensitive* this week to natural opportunities to discuss Christianity. Try to talk with at least one of the people on your list. You need not say much. Just the odd word here or there is sufficient. Do not think you are expected to deliver a polished, theological statement on the nature of Christianity! Just be sensitive and be honest. (During the next group session, you will have opportunity to discuss your attempt to share with others.)

4
Designing Small Group Outreach: The Process of Planning

I am obliged to bear witness because I hold, as it were, a particle of light, and to keep it to myself would be the equivalent to extinguishing it.
Gabriel Marcel

Is sharing the faith solely up to the individual, an individual responsibility? No, witness is a *community* venture. True, each Christian ought to work at becoming an effective Christian conversationalist. Still, the most effective witness so often springs from the *community* of believers. Today, some of the deepest and most significant witness occurs when a small group of Christians and non-Christians meet together to discuss Christianity.

A friend of mine, concerned about his circle of friends, had spoken on many occasions with these business and professional people about Christianity. They were interested in varying degrees. Yet none of them had come to grips with the reality of Jesus Christ. Christianity was only of academic interest to them.

After long thought and prayer, he decided to invite this group to his home to discuss John Stott's *Basic Christianity.* He proposed that they meet once a week, for eight weeks. The reactions of his friends to this invitation varied from real delight to outright fear. But, with only a few exceptions, they came. And they continued to come, week by week, drawn by the vitality of Jesus Christ and by the sheer fun of being together with other like-minded people. By the end of the series, several had decided to follow Christ. Others, who had been dormant Christians for years, rediscovered a vital faith.

Such stories are becoming increasingly common—stories of men and women, on the fringe of Christianity or completely "anti-church," drawn into a small group in which they have the opportunity to consider for themselves the claims of Christ. They then find, to their amazement, that they are drawn into deep commitment to Christ.[1]

The Significance of Small Groups
What is it about a small group that makes it such a splendid means of witness? A number of things. First, a group provides the continuing exposure to Christianity so vital to spiritual discovery. As Sam Shoemaker put it: "Before the average person comes into a vital Christian experience, he usually needs a period of exposure to the experience of others."[2]

Second, because groups are familiar to all of us since we spend hours in informal groups discussing everything under the sun, a group is a natural way of exposing people to Christianity. The same cannot be said of the lecture or sermon. Also, groups generally meet in a familiar place—a home, an office, a favorite restaurant. Consider the implications of this. Which would be easier: to get your neighbors to come to a special series of meetings at your church or to your home for a meal and discussion with several other couples? Your church is an unfamiliar building, full of unknown people following unfamiliar procedures ("Do I stand or kneel now?").

Third, small groups provide opportunity for face-to-face interaction. So often we ask people to consider Christianity without giving them a chance to interact with the presentation. But interaction is necessary if they are to understand how Christ can meet their unique needs.

Fourth, in a successful small group, love, acceptance and fellowship flow in unusual measure. This is the ideal situation in which to hear about the kingdom of God. In this context the "facts of the gospel" come through not as cold propositions but as living truths visible in the lives of others. In such an atmosphere a person is irresistibly drawn to Christ by his gracious presence.

Finally, small groups work because they meet a fundamental need within each of us, the need for fellowship. We all recognize that we need food, air and sleep. But we often forget that what is just as vital to full life is fellowship: deep, meaningful contact with other people.[3]

We need one another. And yet we seem so isolated despite our countless acquaintances. Part of this is due to the barriers we all erect around ourselves to keep others away. Yet we crave the opportunity to drop our mask a little, expose our "true self" and find that we are still loved and accepted.

This can happen in a Christian fellowship group. In fact, this is the nature of an authentic Christian group—a body of people who have faced their dark sides, found forgiveness in Christ and from one another, and are able therefore to live transparently honest lives. A non-Christian, entering such a group, finds the experience virtually irresistible.

As Professor Hans-Ruedi Weber wrote about the early Christians:

The astonishing Christian community life and the Christian service . . . gave the necessary sounding board for the spoken message to become real proclamation instead of empty declaration. . . . Tertullian wrote the following famous words: "Our care for people who cannot help themselves, our works of charity have become a distinguishing mark by which our enemies recognize us: 'See how these Christians love one another,' they say (for they themselves hate one another)." . . . Commenting on this ministering community life of the early Christians, A. Harnack exclaimed: ". . . what power of attraction it must have exercised, as soon as its object came to be understood. It was this, and not any evangelist, which proved to be the most effective missionary."[4]

Small outreach groups also have great value for Christians who want to share their faith. First, it is usually more comfortable to talk about Christ in a small group (which has met together for that purpose), than in a one-on-one conversation. Not only is the topic known and agreed on, but the discussion is not the responsibility of one person only. Invariably a group of Christians will have more wisdom, more insight, more sensitivity and more data than a solitary Christian. In addition, there will often be outside input to enrich the conversation since it is common for a group to listen to a taped lecture together, watch a videotape, read a chapter in a book, or study a passage of Scripture.

Second, the small group is a great place for Christians to learn how to talk easily and comfortably about their faith. If you have not yet verbalized your faith outside of Christian circles, it will be easier to say something in a small group discussion than to launch into a major conversation with your best friend.

The Christian learning to witness will also benefit by watching more experienced Christians share Christ in the small group. I know of no better way and no easier context in which to learn how to be a witness than by participating in small group evangelism.

Finally, the small group provides exactly the kind of support a Christian needs not only when learning to talk about Jesus but whenever doing evangelism. You need your brothers and sisters to pray with you, for you, and for your friends; to support you when you've had a bad time of it; to rejoice with your successes; to hold you accountable for your commitments; and to give you the kind of encouragement we all need when seeking to share Christ.[5]

Planning Small Group Outreach

Being convinced of the value of small group evangelism is one thing. Executing a viable outreach evening is quite another. How is a successful small group outreach planned? What are the decisions that have to be made? Where are the potential problems? Planning for small group outreach will involve decisions in at least five major areas: who to invite, where to meet, when to meet, structure or hospitality, and content.

Target groups. Who will you invite to your small group? This is a crucial question which must be approached with some care, since the composition of the group is vital to its success.

Putting together the right mix. The problem is twofold. First, if people feel uncomfortable in a group because there are not a lot of folk there "like them," then they will be less apt to open up and participate freely. For example, if you have a group composed of two middle-aged professional couples, a teenager, a newly divorced twenty-three-year-old, a retired couple and one family with three children ranging from ages six to fourteen, you will probably spend the whole session trying to break down barriers and establish an easy flow of conversation. On the other hand, a group of nine university students sitting around a room in the dorm will usually talk with ease.

The second problem in "mixed" groups is that the needs are so different. The needs of the young divorced person, for example, who may be in great emotional pain, are probably radically different from the needs of the retired couple who are facing physical and financial problems in the waning years of their lives. Likewise with the teenager who is trying to cope with peer pressure. The best discussion topics are those that arise out of the life needs of the group. Unless your group is reasonably homogeneous, you will be hard pressed to find a common topic.

Homogeneity is not without its problems, of course. One cannot read passages like Ephesians 2—4 or Galatians 3:26-29 without realizing that Christ came to break down barriers between people. The gospel is manifest in the dissolving of these barriers. Certainly this is what the church is all about. But an evangelistic small group is not the church. It is a specific, temporary experience. Social barriers can frustrate the aims of the group by causing people to feel uncomfortable; so that all the group's energy must go into creating relationships and the evangelistic intent of the group is forgotten.

Deciding who to invite. How then do you decide on a target group? The answer is simple: which group are you a part of? With whom do you feel most comfortable? This is the group you should start with.

You must then decide which individuals and couples from this general group you are going to invite. It is important that you begin to pray for these people right away.

But here arises a problem: some Christians have no non-Christian friends. After a seminar on "Using the Home for Evangelism," a middle-aged couple wanted to talk to me. They were quite excited by what had been said. It all seemed to make good sense to them. They were willing to use their home as a center for evangelism. "But," they said, "we've racked our brains to think of people to invite over, and we just don't seem to have any friends outside church circles. What do we do? Can you perhaps send over some interested non-Christians to our house?" At the time I was rather startled by this. But later, when others said the same thing, I realized that this was a real problem.

For many of us, our circle of friends is made up almost exclusively of Christians. Why is this?

There are two factors involved here—one practical and one theological.

On the practical side, it is a simple fact that we make friends at the places where we spend our time. If we devote most of our spare time to church activities, most of our friends will be drawn, quite naturally, from the church. Furthermore, we all feel most comfortable with people who share our viewpoint and hence, as Christians, our real friends tend to be other Christians because we have so much in common with them.

We sometimes go one step further, however, and try to use theology to justify our isolation from non-Christians. The argument goes like this: our Lord himself told us to be in the world, but not of the world (Jn 17:11-19). Hence we must withdraw from all but minimal contact with the "world."

But does that necessarily follow? Does this statement by Jesus really imply that we are to withdraw into a Christian ghetto? I think not, otherwise our Lord would never have told us that we are the "salt of the earth" (Mt 5:13). Salt is a flavoring agent. But it cannot do its job of flavoring until it comes into intimate contact with the food it is supposed to season. Salt is useless if it just sits on the shelf, albeit in a beautiful container.

Often, our Christian groups are just like that—lots of good salt heaped together in a beautiful building, but largely useless, because the salt is not out in the world acting as the flavoring agent.

What then did Christ mean in telling us not to be of this world? Just this: while we live in the world (we have no choice in this really since it is impossible to eliminate contact with non-Christians), we must not be fooled into accepting the world's understanding of itself. We cannot accept the world's value system, ethos or motivation. We must say to the world: "No, the point of life is not money or pleasure or security. The point of life is to know Christ and through him to live in a loving relationship to God and others." Leighton Ford adds,

This "closed corporation" mentality, a sort of Christian isolationism, has been a constant barrier to evangelism. Many Christians have been so afraid of being contaminated by worldliness that they have avoided any social contact with unconverted persons. As a result, they have no natural bridges for evangelism; what witnessing they do is usually artificial and forced rather than the spontaneous outgrowth of genuine friendship.[6]

Now let's return to that list of your non-Christian friends. If it contains only one or two names, your first job is going to be that of seeking to get to know non-Christians. Numerous opportunities exist already: you undoubtedly live surrounded by nonchurch people. You work with non-Christians. Your relatives are probably not all Christians. Resolve, therefore, to get to know the non-Christians who surround you. You will be amazed at their openness to your friendliness and interest. And who knows where your friendship may lead?[7]

One person in your group may have many non-Christian friends. But do not give that person the task of inviting all the outsiders. For in that case, many in the group will not have the experience of inviting others. This is a valuable experience in itself. From it we learn firsthand that nonchurch people are eager to discuss Christianity. Also, if that one person fails, your whole effort is crippled.

Finally, invite more people than you plan for. Last-minute cancellations are not uncommon. And it is better to have too many people than too few. You can always split a large group. Be cautious, though. One group invited eighteen people in order to ensure that five or six would attend. And fourteen people accepted!

Invitations. The crucial factor with invitations is honesty. Never trick a person into coming to an evangelistic group. Not only is manipulation not the loving way to act, it will create tension during the group session. "John, you invited Marge and me to dinner. You didn't tell us that you invited all your Christian buddies as well, and that we are supposed to study the Bible afterward!"

Be candid. You have nothing to hide. Tell your friends exactly what you are doing. "We're starting a weekly group at our home with a few friends from church and some other folks who don't have a strong church commitment but are interested in discussing Christianity. We're beginning next Wednesday. We'll have dinner together and then spend about an hour talking about a passage from the New Testament. We'd love to have you and Marge join us. Incidentally, the first week is really just a trial run. If you find it's not your sort of thing, there are no obligations to come for the whole seven weeks."

When you are forthright in your invitation, your non-Christian friends, by accepting it, are committing themselves to serious participation in the group. They did not have to accept. But they did. They come because they want to.

We often hesitate to invite our friends to groups like this. "Oh, they won't be interested. They won't like it." My experience is quite different. I found that my friends greatly enjoyed the chance to engage in meaningful, purposeful conversation. And it is not only the appeal of serious dialog (versus aimless chit-chat) that is appealing. More and more Americans are out of touch with Christianity. They don't go to church. They never have. So they really don't know much about Christianity. But they are curious. This curiosity is part of a general renewal of interest in America in religion. ("Religion" must be understood here in very broad terms.) Thus the chance to investigate Christianity is welcomed. Even if their interest in Christianity is little more than curiosity about a religious institution and their understanding of the Bible is simply that it is a "great book," this is more than sufficient. Invite them! They will be glad you did. In choosing who to invite, aim at putting together a group half Christian, half non-Christian.

Once you invite folks—in person or over the telephone—it is sometimes wise to follow up with a hand-written invitation containing the details of place and time.

Place

Once you have a sense of *who* you will be inviting, you need to think about *where* you will meet. *Familiarity* is the key criterion. Where will this particular group feel most comfortable? The answer will vary according to the target group. A group of businessmen might feel most comfortable meeting over breakfast or lunch in a private dining room of the local restaurant. A group of teenagers might enjoy the recreation room in a home or at church. University students might use the dorm lounge.

A secondary consideration is the *size* of the room. If you have a choice between a large room which would hold comfortably twice (or more) the number in your group and a small room in which you have to pack people in, *the smaller room* is to be preferred. There is something about being part of a crowd that is conducive to learning.[8]

What you want, if possible, is a room in which your whole group can fit comfortably without squeezing, can sit in a circle, and can see each other's eyes.

Another secondary consideration is *comfort*. If your group is equally familiar with, say, a lounge and a classroom, choose the lounge. A living space is always better than a work or meeting space.

Probably the best place to meet for most groups is in a home. Everybody is familiar with homes. We all live somewhere. We know how to act in people's homes and apartments. We are comfortable in each other's living spaces.

Time

Now that you know who is coming where, you need to decide on *when.* The "when" question has two parts to it. On what day of the week and at what hour will you meet? And how many group sessions will you have?

Again, the crucial question is: What time is best for the schedule of this target group? (This is why it is so important to define your group and to make it homogeneous.) You can meet any time of the day. Look for gaps in the schedule. Perhaps an evening is best. Which evening? Sunday evening? (Beware: more people view television on Sunday evening than any other evening.) You must be both shrewd and sensitive.

The choice of when you meet will determine how much time is available for the group meeting. Two to two and a half hours is ideal. This will give you great flexibility in the content of your sessions. A typical evening might begin at 7:00 P.M., with people actually sitting down by 7:15. The formal meeting would last until 8:30. Refreshments and informal conversation may go on until 9:00 or 9:30 P.M.

Often, the most significant interaction occurs during the informal time afterward. Then, in one-on-one conversation, or in informal groups of three or four, the real issues come out and are discussed. I have found that this spontaneous and meaningful conversation does not generally occur unless there has been a formal group meeting. In other words, do not meet just for "tea and conversation." Without formal discussion, the conversation will probably be merely "how is the weather" chit-chat. It is the small group session itself that provides the content and raises the questions which are later dealt with informally.

Two and a half hours is ideal, but you may have only forty-five minutes. If so, structure your sessions to fit comfortably within the time. Don't fight time limits. You will never have enough time. Simply plan realistically and then stick faithfully to the schedule. Start on time and, especially, end on time. If people expect to be at a group for one and a half hours, they will sit comfortably for that period. If they expect to be there fifty minutes, at about sixty minutes many will be decidedly fidgety. Work with your time limit, not against it.

"But what if we've just got to the good part?" As a rule, go five minutes over your time limit but no more. One principle of good small group leadership is quit while you are ahead. By this I mean, stop on a high note, when everyone *could* go on longer. Don't wait until you have dragged every bit of life out of the topic. The exception to this is when you are involved in deeply personal sharing or crises. Then time is of secondary importance. But even in this case, say to the group: "Our time is up and I know some of you must leave, but it is important for the rest of us to carry on for a while longer."

If you have had a good group meeting, people will stick around—even when the coffee and cake are exhausted. This is one sign that something good is happening in the group.

Another time question is how many weeks should your outreach group meet? It depends on the topic (how much time will you need to cover it?), the group (what is a reasonable length commitment?), and the calendar (what are the natural breaking points? a holiday? the semester's end? the season's conclusion?).

Most people tend to operate in thirteen-week cycles geared to the four seasons. Therefore, it is probably best not to plan a series longer than thirteen weeks. In fact, half a cycle—six or seven weeks—is often an ideal length. Even four sessions (one month) are of value.

A single evening is of value too in deciding whether to continue. You will have the opportunity in the context of the small group training sessions to plan and execute an Outreach Event. Such single events often lead to a series of meetings. In one city, for example, a family invited several friends over to see a "Fact and Faith" film. At the end of the evening everyone so enjoyed it, that a second evening was arranged during which some of the issues raised could be pursued at greater length. This led to a third meeting. Eventually, the group met eight times!

Normally, the greatest benefit comes from a series planned from the start. On several occasions we have conducted Bible studies for businessmen, consisting of one lunch-time study a week for five weeks. We found that men were quite willing to commit themselves to the five weeks—if they knew in advance that it was just for five weeks. An invitation without indication of duration ("We are starting a Bible study on Tuesday. Would you like to come?") is often refused because the person does not know if he is committed for five weeks or five years!

Structure

Once you are clear about *who, when* and *where*, you can turn your attention to planning the meeting itself. What kind of *structure* will you create for the meeting and what will the *content* be? The structural question relates as much as anything to the kind of *food* to be served.

The sharing of food in a social situation is a great way to draw people together. It is central to hospitality. It is not by accident that the key sacrament of the Christian church is organized around the sharing of bread and wine.

Once, in Nairobi, Kenya, we were conducting "home meetings" as part of a citywide preaching mission. Three of us from the mission team had been invited to the home of a rather proper British woman and her somewhat reluctant husband. (She was excited about the mission, he was not.) They had dutifully invited some of their friends (senior British civil servants) and were prepared to listen to whatever we might present. But the situation was quite tense. All the stereotypes were bristling. We were Americans; we were "religious"; we were strangers; and we were not society-types. Our hostess had planned an elegant meal prior to the group meeting itself, and this saved the evening. Something about sharing this meal together, talking around the table, melted away the suspicion. After dinner, we had a congenial discussion about why we were in Nairobi, what we were presenting and who Jesus was. Had we launched straight into our small group interaction without the meal, I am convinced the evening would have been a failure.

So plan your food carefully. There are a great range of possibilities, from a dinner party to light refreshments. Perhaps midmorning coffee is all you need, or a bread and cheese lunch in the office. If you have a teenage group, you could hold a barbecue and swimming party. An easy and enjoyable way to structure an evening is around dessert and coffee. How elaborate or how simple your preparations depends on your target group and where you hold the meeting. What will the group enjoy? What is realistic? What will draw this group together? You may even conclude that food is not necessary at all in this particular situation.

Content
This is the crucial area. You may have done a superb job in planning all the other details. But if people come together and nothing significant happens, all your effort is to no avail.

Message format. How will you present the content that forms the basis for the small group interaction? A rich range of options are available to you.

You may want to show a film to the group and then discuss it. Good films make a great impact. Research by Moody Science films indicates that their films have a greater impact on a small audience than on a large group, and that a series of related films, shown over a period of time, tends to have a cumulative effect.

Or perhaps you will want to play a tape of a lecture or sermon. This can be most stimulating if the material is really good. (Always evaluate materials before you use them.) It is not often that we get to interact with this kind of presentation—we are usually just passive recipients.

Slide shows and filmstrips are also very useful. There are good materials available. Twentyonehundred Productions, the media division of Inter-Varsity Christian Fellowship (233 Langdon, Madison, WI 53703), has productions designed specifically to stimulate discussion about basic life issues and Christianity. The really energetic group might wish to produce its own slide show and then invite friends to its première performance. Another idea, if you are using slides during an evening, is to ask each group member to bring one or two of their favorite slides. Take a few minutes at the beginning of the session to show those slides. In this way, the group will get to know one another better.

Music is another way to provide content for a group. An evening of contemporary music which discusses the dilemma of modern life might be the perfect starting point for discussion. (Be sure to provide copies of the lyrics so everyone can follow the words.) There is a wide range of Christian music available today which can be juxtaposed to problem-setting secular music.

Or you can use a videocassette or videodisc to present your content. For example, *Chariots of Fire* is available to rent quite inexpensively in videocassette, and would generate good discussion (though its length might be a problem). You might even choose to watch a television program together, since certain programs lend themselves to discussion.

Thus far I have discussed only electronic media. I started here because we live in a media-oriented society, and the idea of listening to or watching something with a group and then discussing it is highly appealing. Experiment.

Speakers also provide good content. It is really appealing, for example, to invite the pastor—not to give a sermon but simply to field questions ("everything you ever wanted to know about Christianity but were afraid to ask"). Or invite an "expert" to give a brief presentation and then lead a discussion. A Christian family counselor, for example, could lead a fascinating discussion. Or a Christian professor talking about how she integrates her faith with her discipline would be of great interest. Group members might prepare a special presentation. It is crucial that any and every speaker see this as an opportunity *not* to lecture, but to lead a discussion.

Or you could plan a meeting around an event. Some years ago my wife and I invited a group of friends to celebrate C. S. Lewis's birthday. After cake and coffee, we spent the evening reading aloud and discussing excerpts from his many books. We also used the anniversary of Martin Luther King's birthday to discuss the political and social implications of the gospel. Special events of this sort have great appeal, but they do require extra work and creativity.

When it comes right down to it, often the best medium is the Bible itself. The Bible is rich, fascinating and largely unknown to most of our contemporaries. And of course the Bible is the standard for defining Christian realities.

Serious Bible study appeals to many today—especially if this study is an exercise in self-discovery and is not just a lecture. The Bible will speak for itself. There is one problem, however. The Bible is "our" book. Christians know it. We love it. We seem even to understand it. And sometimes non-Christians are intimidated when they try to study it with us. From their point of view, we know so much about the Bible, who are they to venture an opinion? So they are silent. Great care must be taken to ensure that what you do is true *group* study in which all can participate.

Topics. So far I have said little about topics. Films, tapes, speakers and Bible study can be used to explore a variety of ideas. But the real question is, which topic is appropriate for your group?

Again the answer depends on the target group itself. What are its needs, interests and aspirations? For young married couples who have begun to think about having children, "A Christian View of the Family" could be a stimulating topic. A group of midlife professional people might rather discuss topics related to the issue of meaning and purpose in life, since this relates to needs they feel.

You might also choose a general topic such as "What Christians Believe," "Who Is Jesus?" "Does God Exist?" "Problems in Daily Living," "What Christians Believe and Why," "Learning to Love," or others.

If you pick a topic of real interest to the group, the interaction will be rich. Make sure, however, that the topic interests the non-Christians and not just the Christians in the group!

The Planning Process

At this point in our process of learning about small group evangelism your assignment is to plan *one* meeting. In chapter 8 there is further information on how to plan a series of meetings. Be sure to set aside adequate time for planning. You may have to get together for an extra session; or you might be able to do what needs to be done by phone. Do not simply assign the tasks of planning different aspects of the evening to group members and then expect it all to come together during the event itself. Lack of coordination tends to bring many unwanted surprises!

In this planning process, there may be tension between those group members who need to know *exactly* what will happen at each point in the evening and those who prefer to "play it by ear." Experience shows that it is best to let the "planners" have their way. Otherwise, their level of discontent and fear will be too high for them to participate usefully during the Outreach Event. The best strategy is to plan as well as possible, then be flexible during the event itself so as to adapt to the need and mood of the group. To do this, you will need to designate a leader beforehand, someone whose responsibility it is to initiate experiences, keep the group on track and watch the clock.

Don't try to do too much in one evening (a common mistake). It is better to have two or three really effective interactive exercises than five or six rushed efforts. And make sure your topic is not too broad. One group actually tried to deal with "The Meaning of Life" in two hours!

Remember that you have fairly limited objectives for this Outreach Event. Seek to raise the question of the truth and significance of Christianity in such a way as to whet the interest of people for the Outreach Series which follows. You will discover, as others have, that the best formats are the most direct. People want to get at the real issues—not politely talk around them.

During the sessions, make sure everyone is introduced to everyone else. Providing name tags is often appreciated, even by those who complain about having to wear them. It is important to try to keep the evening flowing smoothly; for example, do not let dinner linger too long.

Most people will enjoy the experience. I have yet to hear that any invited friend has had a bad time. Typically, friends ask: "When can we do this again?" In fact, the most uncomfortable people (if there are any) are the Christians, worrying about all kinds of reactions that seldom occur. Relax and enjoy the experience!

A Sample Outreach Event*
This is the first of what could become a series of small group meetings at Mather House, one of the residential complexes at Harvard. As such the aim of the Outreach Event is to provoke interest in the topic of wholeness in order to suggest a series of follow-up meetings designed to explore various aspects of wholeness.

    I. Target: Students who live and eat at Mather House.

   II. Place: One of the private dining rooms at Mather. Such "tables," organized around a theme, a speaker, or a concern, are a standard feature of house life.

  III. Time: An extended meal time:
                 5:30-5:45 Gather and eat
                 5:45-6:00 Welcome/Introduction of topic/Introduction of each person
                 6:00-6:45 Discussion
                 6:45-7:00 Summary by leader

  IV. Hospitality: The normal evening meal

   V. Content: This will be a free-flowing discussion around a series of carefully chosen questions on the topic: "What does a Whole Person look like at Harvard?" The leader (in this case the Inter-Varsity staff worker) will provide initial comments, guiding questions, a case study, some statistics, and the summary statement. He will also explain his "bias" for Jesus Christ and how a relationship with Christ provides the foundation for wholeness.

*The above example is from Doug Whallon, the Northeast Regional Director for Inter-Varsity Christian Fellowship.

Interaction
Prayer
"To communicate Christ to others, we must communicate with Christ ourselves." Communication with Christ implies a relationship with him. So it must be. In our witness we are not telling others about an intriguing religious figure from the first

century. We are telling them about a living person whom we know.

But this is where the problem lies. For all sorts of reasons, we often let this relationship with Jesus dry up. We either live without any real awareness of his presence (it is possible, he does not force himself on us); *or* we let our relationship with him lapse into a set of duties which we mechanically perform.

Often the core problem is that we stop talking with Jesus. I mean this quite literally. If Jesus is a living person (and he is, the resurrection is a fact of history) and if he can be known by us (and he can be), then for there to be any ongoing relationship, there must be dialog. We must speak to him and we must listen as he speaks to us. Conversation with Jesus is the foundation of our spiritual life. In fact, it *is* our spiritual life.

Try an experiment, won't you?—an experiment in conversing with Jesus.

First of all, find a place where you will be undisturbed for at least fifteen minutes. If this is not true of where you are now, find another place or wait until it is quiet. Do not try to go on until you can be alone and undistracted.

Now, get out a pen and some paper. Then read these verses slowly, listening to Jesus:

Abide in me, and I in you. As the branch cannot bear fruit by itself, unless it abides in the vine, neither can you, unless you abide in me. I am the vine, you are the branches. He who abides in me, and I in him, he it is that bears much fruit, for apart from me you can do nothing. . . . If you abide in me, and my words abide in you, ask whatever you will and it shall be done for you. (Jn 15:4-5, 7 RSV)

This is Jesus speaking to you. Reread this passage, listening carefully to what he is saying to you within these verses and within yourself. Write down what he says. Listen some more. Respond to him. Let him heal you. Let him love you.

Share what has happened in this experiment with someone else.

5
Understanding
Group Dynamics:
The Interactions
of a Small Group

The world today is not impressed by the Bible, or by the Church, or by
preaching. And we cannot confront a needy world with God's love primarily
by these means. The climate of our time is one in which people listen most
readily to laymen with whom they can identify.
Bruce Larson

S mall groups have been acclaimed by some as the answer to
most of the church's ills in this century. But are they? Do
problems just melt away in the face of the dazzling love and
fellowship which the small group invariably generates? The
answer is obvious. We need only recall our own experiences to realize
that there are unsuccessful as well as successful small groups.

Groups do not work automatically. Listen, for example, to the
experience of one couple who work as small group consultants:

Recently we visited a large Midwestern Church where our hosts,
the leaders of about thirty small groups, were sold on the idea of
such fellowships and what they could accomplish for their
church. . . . These leaders believed that if they simply gathered
together to discuss their problems the Holy Spirit would be there,

that the group would take fire, and that the whole community would feel its impact. But this had not happened. The enthusiasm that had carried them through the first months was dying, and the whole experiment was about to collapse.[1]

What had gone wrong? Investigation revealed that the groups had no realistic plan to follow. They simply met. So they floundered.

Groups fail for a variety of reasons. Some, because certain people in the group are hindering it. In others, the leader may be the problem. But there is always a reason. "There is an important rule of thumb, tested by research: *When informed attention is paid to group processes, the chances increase that a group will be able to reach maturity and fulfil its potentialities.* On the other hand, when a group ignores the dynamic processes that influence its life, the chances increase that those dynamics may block the group at some crucial point."[2]

What then are some of these principles of group dynamics which are relevant to the outreach groups you are planning?

Two Levels

The first principle is this: groups function on two levels—the *objective* and the *subjective*. And unless these two levels complement one another, the group will have problems.

The objective side of a group is defined by its task or purpose, be it to study Mark's Gospel, to view a film, or to decide on the budget for next year's church program. In your training group, the objective level is your intention to learn how to use small groups to reach others for Christ.

The subjective side of the group is defined by the emotions, prejudices, needs and private goals of each person and how these influence the group's interaction—the dynamic of inner needs with the intra-group relationships. Invariably, at some point each group member silently asks: "What is my position in this group? Do the others like me? Can I really say what I think? How can I get my way? How can I get the group to see that I am brilliant, or beautiful, or witty, or kind, or spiritual?" Interaction within a group on the level of feelings and needs is the subjective side of group functioning.

Until group members answer these questions, they are not free to get on with the group's task. This is why some groups never seem to accomplish anything. They start out to study Isaiah 53, but then only get through the first two verses. Or they try to plan the forthcoming youth service, but after an hour and a half, the only thing decided is to invite the regular organist to accompany the hymn singing.

Instead of getting on with the task, the group members argue with one another. Or there is a lot of horseplay. Or everyone tries to talk at once—or no one talks at all!

Why is this? What is happening in such a situation? Simply this: the group is failing to concentrate on its task because the *intragroup relationships* have gone wrong.

In short, to be successful a group must pay attention not only to its objective side—its task—but to its subjective needs. A group which concentrates blindly on its task is in danger. Sooner or later, group relationships will frustrate the accomplishment of the objective goal.

Let me illustrate what I mean. A group may be studying (let us say) Mark 2. The leader declares in a rather firm and decisive tone, "Well, it is *obvious* that the first thirteen verses are *just* the story of *another healing* on Jesus' part, so consequently we can move on straightaway to the rest of the chapter. Now, if you will all turn to . . ." At this point Kurt, a member of the group, interjects, in a rather exasperated tone, "But you have missed the point again. That passage is not just about a healing."

Now on the objective level this is fair enough. Kurt is right. The leader is passing too easily over a highly significant incident in Christ's self-revelation. In a healthy group, Kurt's insights would help everyone see more clearly what Mark 2 is about and the leader would welcome his contribution.

But in this situation, both the leader and Kurt are clashing on the subjective level. The leader is saying, by his tone and manner, as well as by his words: "I want all of you to recognize that *I* am the leader and that I can move the group in whatever direction I choose." Kurt is challenging this assumption by exploiting the leader's error, saying, "You have done it again. You are always missing the point. You are a bad leader." Because of the tension between them, the value of the study is lost. The group will never get at Mark 2, because they are so busy getting at each other!

Dealing with Group Tensions

It is a key principle of group dynamics that when interaction on the objective level and interaction on the subjective level are at cross-purposes, the group is in trouble.

For one thing, you must learn to detect quickly that there are problems on the subjective level. You do this by becoming aware of what others are feeling. Perhaps the surest way to know what is going on in a group on the subjective level is to ask *yourself:* "What am *I* feeling right now?" If you are feeling upset, irritated, or defensive, something is wrong. However, these feelings will seldom be expressed directly on a verbal level. People communicate their inner reactions in all sorts of ways—by facial expressions, gestures, tone of voice, level of attention. We must learn to become sensitive to the meaning of these unspoken innuendos. We do not *say:* "I am bored by all this." Rather we just stop taking part in the discussion. Or we slump down in our chair. Or we begin staring at the trees outside the window. In each of these ways we are communicating by means other than words what we are really feeling. Be assured that the group member asleep in his chair is trying to tell you something!

Sometimes our words even *contradict* our feelings. Take the man "who insists in a loud voice, with his teeth clenched and his face nearly purple: 'I am not angry!' "[3]

Second, once the problem has become apparent, the only way to deal with it is to bring it out into the open. After the meeting, over refreshments, you could chat with the person involved. "Margy, I felt that perhaps you were bothered by what went on tonight?" If Margy will express what she was feeling, she can begin to cope with it. It may be possible to ask this same question while the group is still together. ("I sense that some of you are feeling upset.") What Margy is feeling, others may be feeling. Once these subjective feelings are expressed, they can be of value to the group and they will not be destructive. It is not uncommon for the most profitable times in a group to occur when attention is shifted away from the objective to the subjective.

For example, one Sunday in an adult class it was obvious that one of the women in the group, a single school teacher, was bothered. She normally took an active part in the discussion, but on this day she was virtually silent. She seemed particularly pale and withdrawn. Finally, the leader of the group asked her if something was wrong. With that, she burst into tears and spilled out the story. Her mother, with whom she lived, had just been taken to the hospital. While it appeared that the mother would probably recover, the incident had nevertheless aroused all sorts of old fears about the future and how she could cope alone in the world if her mother died. The lesson on the minor prophets that Sunday was quickly forgotten. The group which hitherto had not been particularly close was drawn together in a new way in real love and concern for her. During the next week people had her to dinner; others visited her mother in the hospital. From this point on, the group came alive. They began to discover one another as people. They had been transformed into a loving fellowship, whereas previously they were merely an academic study group—all because one woman had revealed her real feelings.

In this case, the problem arose from outside the group. It may, of course, happen that the problem emerges from within the group itself. An example of this is the power struggle between Kurt and the leader which was mentioned earlier. In either case, the way to cope is to bring the problem out into the open so it can be seen for what it is and then dealt with. (A word of caution is necessary at this point. A group must not be tempted to try to become a therapy group unless there is professional leadership. In a true therapy group there is a deliberate attempt to bring hidden feelings and fears to the surface so people can learn to cope with them. This is something which can only be done successfully by an expert. Great harm can result if a group deliberately releases these inner forces and yet does not know how to cope with them.)

Almost inevitably, out of such situations which seem so disruptive, we learn deeply valuable lessons—about ourselves, about relationships, about conflict and about love, forgiveness and honesty. In other words, we learn in *experience* the meaning of the words we have hitherto just talked about. This is one of the chief values of a group.

Must all groups go through a crisis in order to be drawn together on a subjective level? I don't think so. If a small group pays attention to group-building during its initial sessions, confrontation may not develop.

How do you mold a group of strangers into a real fellowship? There is no quick and easy answer. The best way to begin moving in this direction, however, is by providing ample time for sharing personal histories. If you can do this in such a way as to integrate the personal histories into the topic of the evening, all the better.

For example, you began your first session together as a group by answering three questions about yourself: who are you (facts about your job, studies or daily activity)? what do you enjoy? and when did your relationship with God take off? In this way you said to the rest of the group: "This is who I am." Likewise the group, by its interest, said back to you: "Glad to get to know you. We like having you as part of us." All were given opportunity to talk about the subject they know best—themselves.

Did you notice how the third question related directly to the objective intention of the group session? The point of your training group is to learn how to introduce others to the same experience of the living God that you have had. By hearing how group members met God, the first lesson in this process was learned, namely, that God meets people in a variety of ways.

The implication is that in your small group evangelism, you must provide time for history-giving. This is not a "waste of time," as people sometimes perceive it. But without such personal sharing, you may never get to your task except in the most superficial way. Some small group experts suggest that during initial group meetings you may need to devote sixty to ninety per cent of your time to meeting subjective needs. While different groups get to their tasks quicker than others, the principle is the same. You will save yourself much grief if you pay attention to relational needs.

Patterns of Interaction

The second major principle of group dynamics is this: *People will act in certain predictable ways when they are in a small group.* Some of these behaviors will help or hinder a group, depending on how we respond to them. Let us look at some of these types of group behavior, asking ourselves what this behavior does to a group, and how it can be dealt with if it is harmful. As you read this section, keep in mind the Outreach Event and the Outreach Series which you are going to run in the near future. This will help you understand the sort of people who will be coming into these. This material will also help you understand how you function in a group!

In almost every group there will be the *overtalkative* person who makes long and frequent speeches and expresses opinions on every subject. Such people can be a real help to a group, particularly if they have good ideas. They keep the group going. On the other hand, overtalkative people can hinder a group by hogging too much of the time and by dominating the group. The leader can keep this from happening by addressing questions *by name* to other people. Or the leader might say: "John, hold that comment for a moment and let's see what Mike and Louise feel about this." If this is not effective, the leader may eventually have to speak to the talkative person after a group session to explain how his or her behavior is hindering the group.

Most groups will also have *shy* people. For whatever reasons, such people attend the group without ever really participating. Shy people, however, are useful to a group too. From the sidelines, they can bring an objective perspective into a heated debate. If they will speak up. But this is the problem. Often, because they will not express themselves, their insights are lost to the group. Shy people may inhibit group sharing on a meaningful level because no one really knows what they are thinking and feeling.

Often shy people feel they have nothing of value to contribute. But of course they *do*. Each person is important and has a valuable perspective which the group needs. The group must help shy people understand this. A shy person can usually be drawn out with simple (though not simplistic) questions which require the expression of an opinion or a choice (not questions they would have difficulty answering).

When normally active people withdraw from the group, and become *observers*, it usually means something. They may be upset with the group or distracted by personal problems. The leader should try to draw an observer gently back into the group just as he or she would a shy person.

A *comic's* humorous asides and comments may be very valuable for the group, by providing relief from tensions and a fresh perspective on a debated issue. A good laugh is immensely valuable. But comedy can become a nuisance if it turns *everything* into a joke. Such behavior then becomes just an attention-getting ploy. Furthermore, a flippant comment at the wrong moment can destroy the group atmosphere. If this happens, a chat after the group session may help the person to see that the positive value of his or her humor is being lost, because its frequency makes it annoying.

The person with a *hidden agenda* can disrupt a group. Such a person attends a group ostensibly to participate in the group task, but all the time has something else in mind which is of greater importance. For example, someone may have a date for dinner as soon as the group finishes, and so is eager to bring the business to an end. Another may be more interested in demonstrating her expertise in an area than in getting on with the task. It is difficult to draw such people into the real activity of the group, unless they are willing to be honest about their preoccupations. The leader, sensing someone has a hidden agenda, could ask (if the person can take it): "Tom, something appears to be on your mind. Should we talk about it before we carry on with this discussion?"

The *side-tracker* disrupts by preventing the group from concentrating on the main issues. "That is very interesting, Mary. Now what does the group think about the question at hand . . ." is one way of handling diversions. If a person persists, the leader can offer to discuss the diversionary issue after the session. Sometimes the whole group *welcomes* a tangent, especially if what is being discussed is challenging to them personally. Rather than face such issues, they prefer to retreat into safe side issues.

The *argumentative* person, who disputes every observation, is often baffling to a group. Disagreement, of course, is not necessarily bad. Those who have the ability to see the other side of an issue can save a group from one-sidedness. But the group must feel that the opposition is genuine and not just for the sake of opposition.

Sometimes disagreement occurs simply because a person has not understood what is being said. There is always a gap between what we say and what is heard. Hence a person may be striking out against a caricature. In such cases, the group must patiently help the arguer to "hear" what is really being said. Remember your exercise in reflecting back? However, a person may still disagree. This is well and good as long as the disagreement is good-natured, sincere and respectful. Argument is harmful when it becomes charged with emotion and with the unspoken (but nevertheless communicated) attitude: "If you disagree with me, you are an idiot." This will not happen, of course, if the group has developed a love and respect for one another.

Group Atmosphere
In fact, many problems on the subjective level will be avoided if the group atmosphere is right. If people feel warmth, love and acceptance from a group, they will not have to argue ruthlessly or talk too much. If they feel that they will be accepted and not condemned no matter what they say, they will not have to conceal themselves by being either shy or boisterous. If the group sets the example of honest sharing, everyone will be encouraged to drop the mask behind which they hide and let their true selves be known in the group. In this way too they will be opened up to the healing, redemptive love of Christ.

What atmosphere then do we want to strive for? To my mind, the answer is summed up in three words: acceptance, honesty and love. Aim to be an *accepting* group—not a judgmental group always ready to pounce on a person's faults or wrong ideas; an *honest* group—a group where true feelings and thoughts can be expressed, where real growth can take place; and a *loving* group—in which there is a genuine caring for one another.

Acceptance. As long as we consider ourselves to have "arrived" spiritually or to have special insight into God's will which few others share, we will stand in judgment of others. Consciously or unconsciously, we will judge the non-Christians in the group because they have not yet arrived at our state of spiritual understanding. Hence, we feel that non-Christians must learn from us and that we cannot learn from them. Often, we also judge those Christians who are not of our denomination (or group). They obviously have little spiritual wisdom or they would be in our church!

We become loving, accepting persons only when we understand that we too are sinners in need of grace. And we need the grace of forgiveness not just once, at our conversion, but over and over again. Until we reach this point, we will tend to stand as judges to other people. We will evaluate their ideas and behavior on the basis of our ideas and behavior which we consider normative. We can only do this because we have never really seen ourselves as God sees us—with our pretense, blind spots, unadmitted failings and other failings. As Dietrich Bonhoeffer has said: "If my sinfulness appears to me in any way smaller or less detestable in comparison with the sins of others, I am still not recognizing my sinfulness at all."[4] May God grant each of us a vision of just how deep and all-pervasive in us is this flaw called sin. And may he also grant us the knowledge of how rich his forgiveness is in the face of our great need.

What happens then when we come to the point of really believing ourselves to be men and women with deep needs? For one thing, we can begin to allow God to meet these needs in us and hence we start to experience the reality of the gospel. Second, we will start accepting all people, Christian and non-Christian, as they are, as fellow sinful creatures. Not that we therefore accept sin. On the contrary, we find a new and deep abhorrence of this cancer because we know how it destroys. Third, we find a new rapport with others because we come to them, not as one who has "arrived," but as one beggar telling another beggar where to find food.[5] And we will see other beggars joyously discovering that "food" for themselves. Sam Shoemaker summed it all up when he wisely said: "It takes a sinner to catch a sinner."[6]

Honesty. Once we have seen ourselves as we really are (sinful people who are nevertheless loved by God), then we not only begin to drop our judgmental natures, but we also can become honest.

We begin to develop a faculty for honesty when we become aware of our own sinful nature. As we face our real selves (and go on facing ourselves) and then allow Christ to forgive us and heal us and make us new, we become able to live with the dark side of our personality. It is only when we cannot face this side of ourselves that we have to pretend it does not exist, and hence we are forced to be dishonest. But *we can face anything in ourselves if we know that God really loves us; that where there is real guilt we will find deep forgiveness; and that our shadow side can be redeemed.* Love, forgiveness and redemption wipe away the effects of the dark thing and give us a transparency before others which is the mark of honesty.

When we have seen ourselves for what we are and have allowed Christ to deal with us, then we can open ourselves to others. And when we open up ourselves, others can begin to open up themselves to us. This is the first step to their own healing. "In all of his recent books Tournier (the Swiss psychiatrist) indicates that when he is personally willing to share his own faults and doubts and failures with his patients . . . and make himself vulnerable to them, healing takes place. But when he is merely professional and sits back and asks the patient to expose his problem, he does not see the same results."[7]

This is why honesty is essential to a group. If we are all pretending to feel what we do not feel, or if we hide behind pious words or ideas, nothing can happen. The Holy Spirit is bound by us. The power of the gospel is inhibited. But when we can be open, particularly with what our experience of Christ has been, life can flow.[8]

One more note. One man has written: "Transparent honesty is only possible for persons who are emotionally and spiritually healthy and mature."[9] He is, of course, right. Our outreach groups will reflect the richness—or poverty—of our spiritual experience. What this says once again is that it is top priority for each of us to devote ourselves to knowing Christ. The starting point in our attempt to be honest may have to come when we honestly admit that we know little of Christ. But once we have faced this, let us then resolve to rectify the situation.

Love. Love is the inevitable consequence of acceptance and honesty. When you find that people know the real you (because you have been honest) and still accept you (with warts and all), what you feel is love.

Of course, love is more than a feeling. Christian love *(agape),* by definition, is active, disinterested action on behalf of another. Still, it is on the feeling level that love strikes home and changes us. It is truly awesome to be part of a small group where love is both experienced in concrete form and felt within on a deep level.

What I have been outlining here is the *ideal:* a group in which each person is honest and accepting, warm and outgoing to all; a group in which posturing of any sort is unnecessary; a group in which the subjective and objective levels of interaction work in harmony; a group in which the needs of individuals are met and in which they come to experience the reality of the gospel.

Your group will not be perfect, any more than you or I will be perfect. I find it much easier to *write* about honesty, acceptance and nonjudgment than to *act* consistently in this fashion with my family, friends and colleagues. But this is my goal—to become free in Christ to be what he wants me to be.

So too, what I have outlined in these pages are *goals* (and some ideas about reaching them). They are not standards by which you must judge your group. They are what you aim for.

Much more could be said about setting up and running small groups. However, the way you will learn most about conducting small groups is by being a part of small groups yourself. Your own experience in groups is your best textbook. All I can do is to give you some idea of how to start and what to watch for.

Interaction

The Small Group and Me

You have been in a group now for four weeks. It is time to stop and take stock of your relationships with others in the group. This will be a valuable exercise, for our relationships with others in a group often mirror our relationships with people in general. If you are not going through this book with a small group but on your own, think back to other small group experiences you have had as you answer these questions.

1. What sort of group member are you? Check those descriptive phrases below which best describe how you act in your small group.

a. Shy .... _____	k. Summarizing .... _____
b. Overtalkative .... _____	l. Bored .... _____
c. Argumentative .... _____	m. Enthusiastic .... _____
d. Witty .... _____	n. Fearful .... _____
e. Aggressive .... _____	o. Baffled .... _____
f. Passive .... _____	p. Hostile .... _____
g. Looking on .... _____	q. Hidden agenda .... _____
h. Silent .... _____	r. Peacemaker .... _____
i. Theorizing .... _____	s. Gatekeeper .... _____
j. Leading .... _____	t. Other .... _____

2. Why do you suppose you function this way?

3. Which roles do you play in the small group and how does your presence benefit the group?

4. What are the potential problems?

5. What aspect of your group behavior would you like to change? Why?

6. How can you do this?

7. How do you think others in this group view you?

8. Do you have problems relating to anyone in the group? Why?

9. What can you do to improve these relationships?

10. How would you rate yourself as an honest person?

11. How would you rate yourself as an accepting person?

12. If you dared to be totally honest with one other person, what would you share?

13. From your relationship in the group, what have you learned about your relationships to your family? your friends? your colleagues?

6
Talking about Jesus: The Content of Our Witness (I)

During the Tell-Scotland campaign in the mid-fifties, a minister from
the north wrote to the organizers at the movement's headquarters in
Glasgow. "We have our committees organized, our literature prepared, our
schedules set, our promotion underway. We are ready now to take part in
'Tell Scotland.' But, pray tell me, what are we to tell Scotland?"
Leighton Ford

Your Outreach Event has come and gone. One question which
surely crossed your mind prior to the event was this: what
exactly should we be trying to communicate about Christianity? No specific answer was given to this question because
you had quite enough to worry about simply planning and executing
the Outreach Event. Furthermore, the Outreach Event was not
intended to do more than rouse interest in Christianity. If people
went away saying, "You know, maybe there is something to
Christianity after all," then you were more than successful. It is a
different story, however, when it comes to the Outreach Series. These
are the meetings which you will be planning and hosting after this
training group finishes in three more weeks. Then, when you have

more time (several meetings, not just one), you will want to present the full gospel message. In this chapter and in chapter 7, we will focus on the content of the gospel and how it might be communicated in a small group setting.

It is important, first of all, to have an overview of the gospel message. What are the key elements of this "good news" which we hope to present to others? I have an exercise I do with my students in which I ask them to jot down what they consider to be the key words which define the essence of the gospel. Then I ask, "What would you want to talk about should an interested, unconverted friend ask you to explain Christianity?" After a few minutes I collect responses. Typically I will end up with a list of no less than twenty-five or thirty "big words"—that is, words like *faith, salvation* and *justification* that are laden with content. It takes only a moment's reflection to see that there is simply not time in an ordinary conversation to explain all these concepts. So I ask again: "What are the really foundational elements?"

Eventually it becomes clear that at the core of the gospel is Jesus and what he has done to address the human condition. The following diagram is one way of expressing these central affirmations of the Christian faith. The diagram is not perfect, complete or the only way

A Gospel Outline

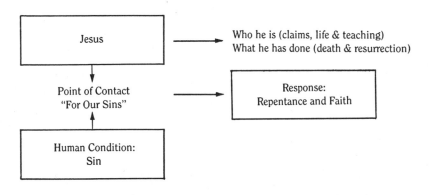

of communicating the gospel. This formulation and others like it are merely ways of helping us to get a grasp on the key things that must be said. They also help us not to get lost in the maze of all the other things that might be said.

Notice the three main parts. First, the gospel message focuses on *Jesus*. He is central. He is at the core of what God is doing in the world. Second, Jesus' life was not lived in a vacuum nor without purpose. Rather his life, death and resurrection addressed the central problem of the human condition: namely, *sin*, which has cut us off from God and from each other. Finally, any gospel presentation must connect together the first two facts. How does God's action in Jesus Christ answer our need for forgiveness from our sin? Specifically, how does a man or woman *respond to Jesus Christ?* The first element of the paradigm—the nature and work of Jesus—will be addressed in this chapter. In chapter 7, the question of sin and the nature of our response to Jesus will be the topics.

Jesus is the heart of the gospel. Our ultimate aim in all witness and evangelism is to help others discover who he is in such a way that they are drawn irresistibly to him. In particular, we need to present the answers to two questions: Who is Jesus? and What has he done?

The Person of Jesus
There is much confusion over just who Jesus is. If you asked a representative sample of people who Jesus is, their responses would range from prophet to lunatic, from religious fanatic to gentle shepherd. They would see him as a great teacher, as a seer with deep insight into the nature of reality, as a figment of pious imaginations, as a kindly but misguided fraud, or as the Son of God. It is important, therefore, that when we present the gospel, we do not simply use the name *Jesus* and expect people to understand him as we do.

In presenting who Jesus is, it is often best to begin with Jesus' own understanding of who he is. Specifically, we need to help others see that Jesus claimed to be "the Son of God." C. S. Lewis put this well:

Jesus said: "I am the begotten of the One God, before Abraham was, I am," and remember what the words "I am" were in Hebrew. They were the name of God, which must not be spoken by any human being, the name which it was death to utter. . . . If you had gone to Buddha and asked him, "Are you the son of Brahma?" he would have said: "My son, you are still in the vale of illusion." If you had gone to Socrates and asked, "Are you Zeus?" he would have laughed at you. If you had gone to Mohammed and asked, "Are you Allah?" he would first have rent his clothes and then cut your head off. If you had asked Confucius, "Are you Heaven?" I think he would have probably replied: "Remarks which are not in accordance with nature are in bad taste."[1]

Jesus set himself apart from all other prophets and teachers by the magnitude of his claims. People must understand this fact if they are to come to him. We dare not avoid the issue.

"I am ready to accept Jesus as a great moral teacher, but I don't accept His claim to be God." That is the one thing we must not say. A man who was merely a man and said the sort of things Jesus said would not be a great moral teacher. He would either be a lunatic—on a level with the man who says he is a poached egg—or else he would be the Devil of Hell. You must make your choice. Either this man was, and is, the Son of God: or else a madman or something worse. You can shut Him up for a fool, you can spit on Him and kill Him as a demon; or you can fall at His feet and call Him Lord and God. But let us not come with any patronizing nonsense about His being a great human teacher. He has not left that open to us. He did not intend to.[2]

Who then is Jesus? Most simply stated, Jesus is God. Jesus is God-in-the-flesh, who came at a particular time in human history for a specific purpose, namely, to end humanity's rebellion against God. Only when people know just who Jesus is—Savior and Lord—can they come to him in truth and confidence.

If you are clear and articulate in your witness, it is at this point that your friends will stop and say, "Wait a minute! You can't ask me to believe that! What proof is there that Jesus is actually who he claims to be?" This is a fair question and every inquiring mind must be satisfied about it.

There is, of course, substantial proof for the genuine inquirer that
Jesus is indeed God incarnate. The ultimate verification of Jesus'
claim to deity is the resurrection. John Stott's *Basic Christianity* gives
a splendid survey of the evidence surrounding Jesus' claim to deity.
Michael Green's *The Day Death Died* (InterVarsity Press) deals with
the historical fact of the resurrection.

The Work of Jesus
The next question is: For what purpose did God become human?

He came, of course, to teach us. But important though his teaching
is, he came primarily to die. For in dying he made it possible for
women and men to be forgiven and hence to come into fellowship
with God.

His death was necessary to overcome the barrier between God and
humankind, a barrier resulting from human choice to live life apart
from God, which we call *sin*. When we choose to go it alone, this sin
spoils us, making us unable to know God in a personal way. Through
Christ's death, the spoiling effect of sin is reversed. People can be
forgiven and know God. As Peter said: "Christ died for sins once for
all, the righteous for the unrighteous, to bring you to God" (1 Pet
3:18).

A great deal more could be said about the atonement. Volume after
volume has been written in an attempt to plumb the depths of its
meaning. Yet all that is necessary for us to know and to believe is
that because Christ died, we can come back to God and be forgiven.
Do not complicate your witness by trying to expound theories about
the atonement, since you run the risk of obscuring the obvious and
glorious fact that by Christ's death we can come to God. As C. S.
Lewis put it:

People ate their dinners and felt better long before the theory of
vitamins was ever heard of: and if the theory of vitamins is some
day abandoned they will go on eating their dinners just the same.
Theories about Christ's death are not Christianity: they are explanations about how it works. . . . We are told that Christ was
killed for us, that His death has washed out our sins, and that by

dying He disabled death itself. That is the formula. That is Christianity. That is what has to be believed. Any theories we build up as to how Christ's death did all this are, in my view, quite secondary: mere plans or diagrams to be left alone if they do not help us, and even if they do help us, not to be confused with the thing itself.[3]

But Jesus did not just die and then remain dead. Christians have no tomb of their dead prophet which they visit on a pilgrimage. On the third day after his killing, he rose bodily from the grave. He was alive again—fully and thoroughly. He had a body. (He was not a ghost.) He spoke to people. He ate with them. After forty days, he ascended bodily to heaven. This means that he is still alive and therefore can be known. A relationship with Jesus is possible. Christian faith therefore is not merely the affirmation of a set of doctrinal propositions; nor is it simply conformity to an ethic or membership in an organization. To become a Christian is to come into relationship with the living Christ, who died for our sins and then rose again in triumph over death.

Talking about Jesus

How do you express these truths about Jesus in the context of a small group in such a way that they can be heard?

First, our attitude as Christians is crucial. Do we want *dialog* about Jesus or *monolog*? This is not an easy question to answer. We have strong views about Jesus. We sense that in our culture there is a distorted understanding of his true nature. We want to correct this. We want to "present the facts," "set the record straight." What could a non-Christian contribute to a conversation about who Jesus is? So we lecture and pontificate.

But the fact is, when non-Christians begin to examine the data for themselves, they have amazing insight into who Jesus is. And I have yet to meet a Christian who has got Jesus figured out completely. My understanding of Jesus has grown (and is growing) over the years. He is far more than I ever imagined; and I learn deep lessons about him from the whole of his creation, including unbelievers. So, real conversation about Jesus between a group of Christians and non-Christians is not only possible, it can be highy fruitful to all concerned. The key is to create an environment that promotes respectful and interested inquiry.

There are two ways to do this: *directly* or *indirectly*. The first involves taking a look directly at who Jesus is, whether by books or other media. For example, C. S. Lewis's *Mere Christianity* is a concise, accurate and highly compelling presentation of who Jesus is. Studying it together over a series of meetings could be fascinating for a group. To do this, make sure everyone has a copy. Then agree together to read certain chapters prior to the small group session. (You might want to prepare a series of questions as a study guide to focus this reading.) Then go over the material together during the group session. Prepare a set of fact/meaning/application questions (as described in chapter 8) to guide the discussion. And remember, your aim is not to "convince" as much as it is to "present." Ultimately, it is the Holy Spirit who convinces. Don't take that burden on yourself.

Or, if people do not have time to prepare for small group discussion, you can read the material together—silently or aloud—as a group. Or you might have subgroups work on several different kinds of material—a collection of Jesus' direct claims to deity; a set of materials on his "acted out" claims to deity; and a third set of materials on other people's assessment of his claims. Each subgroup is assigned the task of distilling the material into a five-minute presentation to the whole group. Then use these presentations as the basis for group interaction.

There are ways other than print to present the facts about Jesus. For example, have someone talk for ten minutes about this material and then discuss what has been said. But make sure it is an engaging presentation. You might want to use a lecture or sermon on audio or videotape. Or you may want to use some of the other ideas presented in chapter 4. Choose your medium in accordance with your audience.

However the material is presented, make sure it is done well.

Evaluate carefully whatever material you use. Is it clear? Does it use jargon only Christians will understand? (You may have to develop a sensitivity to how non-Christians "hear" our favorite words like *faith, sin, salvation* and others.) Is it interesting? Does the style of presentation feel "musty" or out of an alien culture (from the non-Christian point of view)? Or is it alive, full of energy? Is there a convicting power to the piece? Does it ring true? Is it full of love? Of course it will probably be impossible to find the perfect material as described here. Still, if you are aware of the drawbacks of a particular piece, you can then compensate for these and not allow them to mute the overall impact.

The *indirect* (or inductive) approach is often the best way to help people discover who Jesus is because it involves examining Jesus indirectly through a topic which is of immediate interest to the group. For example, a subject like "A Christian View of the Family" will reveal that at the very heart of Christianity is family—God's family created by the work of Christ and sustained by the Holy Spirit. To discuss the idea of the family of God leads quite naturally to the whole question of how we come to know God in the first place (and so become a member of his family); of how Jesus' death makes such a relationship with God possible; and of how such family ties are lived out on a daily basis.

This indirect approach can be valuable in that, while discussing topics of high interest to the group, you raise fewer potential barriers (since you are not beginning with a potentially controversial subject like "Did Jesus really rise from the dead?"). The drawback is that it is much harder to make sure that facets of Jesus' person and work are brought out and examined.

To my mind, the best indirect approach involves inductive study of a Gospel account. Your topic is, say, "The Gospel of Mark." In studying Mark the nature and work of Jesus will unfold slowly and quite naturally. And it will present itself in a compelling way. Both Christians and non-Christians will learn, as the answer to the question Who is Jesus? gradually emerges from the text itself.

Whether the approach is direct or indirect, the question remains:

How does a small group digest what it has discovered? Discussion together around a series of carefully crafted questions is one way to do this. Reflection on the personal response to Jesus is a second approach. For example, were one to study the Caesarea Philippi incident in Mark 8:27—9:1 and come upon the question "Who do people say I am?" it would be appropriate to ask, "How does our culture answer that question today?" Then one might ask, "How have *you* answered that question? Who was Jesus to you at five years old? at fifteen? at twenty-five? now?"

Role play is another great avenue to learning. Study the resurrection accounts together. Then ask a group member to act as if she had just been at the empty tomb. First she tries to explain what she saw to three others (who can role play different first-century characters) and then they discuss together how the tomb came to be empty. Role play is powerful. Em Griffin describes his experience of watching high-school students talk themselves into considering Christian faith by a form of role play.

> In a group meeting I'll suggest they list all of the possible benefits that they've heard or that they can think of for being a Christian. I stress that they don't have to actually believe that these things will really come to one who follows Christ, just that they might. I'll then open the meeting up to anyone who wants to throw in an idea. They're completely free to participate or remain silent. Most of these kids aren't Christians, yet they come up with dozens of great reasons why they should trust God. I found that they usually remember best what they said themselves. Often they come to believe it and act upon it.[4]

Small group study of who Jesus is is both fascinating and profitable. The basic process is quite straightforward. First, present the material in a clear and compelling way. Then ponder together and digest what you have found so that it strikes both mind and heart. In this way both Christians and non-Christians are challenged to respond in a new way to Jesus.

Interaction
Evaluating Our Group Outreach
Answer the following questions. (They will serve as a basis for discussion during your small group session.)
1. How would you rate the Outreach Event in terms of:
   a. Interest level:

   b. Communication:

2. Describe the atmosphere of the evening:

3. How did you feel personally:

   a. Before the meeting:

   b. During it:

c. Afterward:

4. What were the best parts of the evening?

5. What parts did not go well?

6. What can be done to improve matters?

7. What lessons did you learn?

A Dialog about Jesus

Write out an imaginary dialog in which a Christian explains to an interested non-Christian (1) who Jesus is, (2) what he has done, and (3) what this means to a person. Be sure to cover each of these three points. Assume that the non-Christian has no objections, but is just ignorant about Jesus. You might want to write this as a dialog between you and the friend you brought to the Outreach Event, or as a letter to a friend who failed to show up at your Outreach Event.

    This dialog will not only give you a chance to think about and write out your answer to this key question; it will also help you to think about the sorts of questions non-Christians actually have about Jesus. If you find it difficult to complete this exercise, you may want to do some reading in either John Stott's *Basic Christianity* or C. S. Lewis's *Mere Christianity*.

7
Introducing Others to Jesus: The Content of Our Witness (II)

The longer I live the more sure I become that nearly everyone needs the jolt and shock of a deep challenge and a real conversion. Behind the "But I always have had faith" attitude lies often great pride: and the sign of it may be this person's powerlessness to get faith across to anyone else.
Samuel Shoemaker

The key question in this chapter is: How can a person become a real Christian? How does a person who has come to *believe* that Jesus is the Son of the living God translate these historical and theological convictions into the *experience* of coming to know Jesus Christ? Christianity lived out on the level of creedal commitment only is often lifeless and joyless. What is it, then, that turns these true assertions into the kind of flaming truth that changes a person's life? An awareness of personal need and lostness. This is the second part of the gospel paradigm (p. 100)—the human condition.

The Human Condition
What *is* the human condition? In a word, we are all flawed. Some-

thing is wrong—radically wrong—with all human beings. To say such a thing is not so outrageous to modern ears. We all know (unless our ideology prohibits us from acknowledging it) that there is a sickness within us. We see this sickness expressed on a planetary level in persistent wars, in worldwide hunger, and in pollution that threatens the very existence of the biosphere necessary to sustain life. We see this cancer play itself out in hostility on all levels of human society, be it nation against nation, group against group, person against person. Perhaps clearest of all, we know the fact of sin within ourselves. We lie, we cheat, we manipulate, we spoil, we harm, we hate, we weep. It is in our pain, in the context of fractured relationships, out of our disillusionment and despair that we discover our shadow side. And in discovering our own darkness, we are chilled to see that same darkness in others.

This is what the Bible calls "sin." But it is almost impossible to use this word *sin* today, because we have so sanitized it that it has been stripped of most of its meaning. *Sin* has become a euphemism for "gross misdeeds"—like robbing a bank, killing your mother-in-law, or raping a child—the sort of things only the criminal margin of society engages in. We do not think of *ourselves* in this way.

The biblical definition of sin, however, is much deeper, much more comprehensive. In fact, there is not one but a variety of Greek and Hebrew words which are translated into English as "sin." These words can be arranged into two sets, each of which capture a different aspect of sin. One set of words has at its core the idea of *law-breaking.* The central metaphor would be of a field and a fence. To go over the fence and into the forbidden field would be to *transgress;* to do what was not allowed. This set of words focuses on active (and often deliberate) wrongdoing. Here is where robbing a bank falls. Here is where gossip and gluttony fit.

The second set of words has at its core the idea of *failure.* The central metaphor here would involve an archer shooting arrows at a target, none of which hit the bull's eye; they have all *fallen short.* Sin is also like that. It is *not doing,* as well as *wrongdoing.* It is what we fail to do (sins of omission), as well as what we have done (sins of commission). As such, this set of words strikes right at the heart of our human problem. It is not just that we act badly; it is that there is a spoiling principle within us that expresses itself through our failure. Both conditions need fixing. Our faults and our failures bring grief—to us, to others and to God.

Sin and Human Need

How then do we communicate the nature of the human condition in such a way that our non-Christian friends will acknowledge their own need (not continue denying it) and find in Jesus the power to deal with it?

One thing we must not do is point our finger and say, "Look what you did. See what a rotten person you are." People simply clam up or lash out in the face of that sort of guilt-oriented accusation. They cannot help it. God created human beings in such a way that they protect themselves psychologically from such assaults. Jesus himself said, "Do not judge, or you too will be judged" (Mt 7:1). He was speaking, I think, not just of ultimate judgment but of the immediate judgment which comes when we presume to judge others.

We are powerless to bring conviction of sin to another. This is the work of the Holy Spirit. As our Lord said: "When he [the Holy Spirit] comes, he will convict the world of guilt in regard to sin and righteousness and judgment" (Jn 16:8). It is not only presumptuous but highly dangerous for us to attempt to play the part of the Holy Spirit. We end up manipulating people and thus harming them deeply by obscuring the real work of the Holy Spirit.

What we *can* do is to be honest about our own sin and failure. When we are honest and open, others are freed to admit (even if only to themselves) that they too are needy people. But we can go further than this. If accusation creates defensiveness, then affirmation creates openness. It is a curious fact that it is in the context of an affirming situation, when others are pointing out our strengths, that we are free to say: "Yes, but there is this problem. . . ."

We can also pray. We can pray for that inner work of the Holy Spirit in the lives of our friends whereby the scales drop away from their eyes and they "see" the way things actually are.

But what is the purpose of this seeing? Why is it important that we identify our own transgression and failure? Because only when we see our need can we begin to discover its roots. And in seeing the root of sin, we understand why it was essential that "Christ die for our sins."

Let me explain what I mean. You share with a friend about the deep loneliness that you faced as a child growing up in a broken family. (This sharing does not come out of the blue but is in a context where such honesty on your part is appropriate.) You relate how this loneliness carried over into adolescence and adulthood—pushing you into unhealthy relationships that, far from making you less lonely, only reinforced your fear of intimacy. Your friend relates how she too felt the same sort of thing. Not that she was especially lonely as a child but just that given the emotional climate in her family, she never learned how to relate warmly to others. She too knows about inadequate relationships.

In the context of such sharing (notice that what we offer our friend is not "pat answers" but our own pain and suffering), an important thing happens. *Need is named and owned.* As we will discuss, repentance—which is the first step in Christian commitment—begins with awareness of need. A second step is necessary, however. Somehow a connection must be made between our need and God's love. One connection might be in discovering that at the root of our loneliness lies a lack of relationship with God. We were made to know God. And when we stand outside such a relationship there is an inner void that hampers our attempts at developing other relationships. This is to *interpret* for your friend the root reality behind all loneliness. You may do this in an analytic way: "Your loneliness is caused by your longing for God." Or you may do this in an experiential way by simply sharing that in discovering this fact yourself, and then coming to Christ, for the first time in your life you no longer felt lonely.

Other problems find their root in a broken relationship with God. We *fear* because we have no contact with the Lord of the universe who sets limits and boundaries. We *hate* because we have never known the unconditional love of God. We *lust* because for us relationships are getting not giving; because we do not know about God's giving love as shown in Jesus Christ. We feel *lost* because we have no effective contact with the God who gives purpose and direction. It is often helpful to others to interpret theologically the meaning of their experiences—as long as this is done in love with no hint of condescension.

Another connection between our need and God's love is the general truth of the gospel that we can bring all need—no matter what it is—to Jesus Christ and know that he will begin to heal us because he loves us and died for us. Indeed, this is precisely what we want to communicate: that the answer to our sin and failure and brokenness is found in Christ Jesus.

How does this happen? How does Jesus' death answer the problem of sin? According to Mary McDermott Shideler,

There are in general three ways by which an omnipotent God could heal us. With a wave of His hand, so to speak, He could override our divided wills, minds, bodies and hearts. If He did, however, He would destroy our freedom and turn us into slaves or puppets . . . . Or God could prescribe for us a course of action, promulgate a set of rules, which when followed would result in a cure. Many people believe that this is what He has done, and all that He has done, but at best it is a partial measure because its success depends upon what man can do by means of his own efforts. . . .

Therefore, Christianity says, God took a third way in which our sin is not amputated as by surgery, or forced into line as by a brace, but is healed as by medicine. The following analogy should not be pressed too far, but it will serve my immediate purpose. As animals are inoculated with certain viruses in order to develop antibodies that can be made into vaccines, so God voluntarily contracted man's disease of sin, knowing that only he could produce antibodies that would be effective against the disease, and knowing also that the process would require Him to suffer the agony and death that result from sin. He had to be fully man so that the disease could infect Him. He had to be fully God so that He could

develop antibodies for our healing. Only by receiving this vaccine
could men be cured without being irremediably maimed in the
process. It is as simple and as fundamental as that.[1]
Christ died for our sins to enable us to come back to God and hence
to come alive. As Paul put it: "You were spiritually dead through your
sins and failures, all the time that you followed this world's ideas of
living, and obeyed the evil ruler. . . . We all lived like that in the
past. . . . But even though we were dead in our sins God, who is rich
in mercy, because of the great love he had for us, gave us life together
with Christ" (Eph 2:1-5 Phillips). Because of sin, our spiritual nature
is dead. Because Christ died for our sins, we can be made alive.

Discussing Sin in a Small Group
In the context of a small group, this question of sin must be dealt
with on two levels: the theological and the experiential.

On a theological level, we have to assert the reality of sin. We live
in an age of easy tolerance which often obscures the consequences
of our actions. Judging from what we see on TV, for example, adultery
might be distasteful to the old ladies at the bridge club, but between
consenting adults who are attracted to one another, it is good. It is
no big deal. It is "love." We are thus padded from the reality of what
adultery does to a marriage. We are not told about the gut-wrenching
pain it brings to all concerned, including innocent children. We do
not see the price—psychological and even physical—that must
always be paid for such infidelity.

Even less do we see the *spiritual impact* of sin. At the heart of sin
is self-centeredness. "I want it my way. I am lord of my own life."
Thus we dethrone and banish the Lord of all life. Our sin prevents
us from acknowledging this and returning to him. So we walk away
from him. And in walking away from him, we die—slowly, deeply and
finally. By our lifestyle we decide that we do not want to live with
God—now or in eternity. And God honors that decision.

There are many ways to set this theological issue before the group.
A book could be studied, such as *The Abolition of Man* by C. S. Lewis
(or its science-fiction counterpart *That Hideous Strength*), or Book 1

in *Mere Christianity,* "Right and Wrong as a Clue to the Meaning of the Universe." Dostoevsky and Kierkegaard display our lostness with great power and eloquence. Paul does too; the whole reality is there in Romans and Ephesians 2. Modern films (or videotapes), plays and fiction too are often quite good at penetrating our pretensions. Even the better TV programs do this. How did you learn about the meaning of sin? Perhaps that is the appropriate vehicle for the group.

However true it is that we need to comprehend the theology of sin and its consequences, it is even more important that we grasp the reality of sin on an experiential level. We need to see and feel deeply the reality of our own sin. How can this happen in a small group?

Since we cannot convict others of sin, all we can do is create a climate of *openness* and *affirmation,* in which all are free to acknowledge sin. This is possible within a small group. Indeed, this is why small groups are so powerful. But you cannot create such a climate instantly. It must develop over time. The key elements to it are *history-giving* and *active affirmation.* By history-giving I mean that you must build into each group session the opportunity for people to share yet more of their own life history. At the first session you may each answer questions about work and hobbies. At the third session, this sharing may be around warm childhood memories or dreams for the future. By telling our stories to one another, we become more open. There is a certain affirmation simply in sharing an incident—especially a difficult one—and feeling from the group warmth, understanding and acceptance.

But you need to go beyond this and create situations of active affirmation. For example, Lyman Coleman has one exercise called "Strength Bombardment" in which "one person sits in silence while the others think of a particular strength they see in his life. Each in the group then tells the strength he has selected and explains why. For instance one might say, 'Jim, I see the quality of *compassion*—because you have a tremendous ability to care.' Another might say, 'I see in you a quality of childlikeness—because you are beautifully honest and transparent.' "[2]

History-giving and affirmation create the climate within which it becomes possible to name and own personal need. The discussion may begin with "other people." "How is sin experienced today?" Perhaps a stack of newspapers is brought in and each person scans a section in order to locate examples of our "fallenness." "How do people cope with such lostness?" the group leader might ask.

Eventually, shift the questions from the general to the specific. "From this list of problems, which strikes the closest to your own experiences?" Here, the Christians must be willing to be vulnerable (yet without being trite). Here too one can share how Christ has brought healing to pain (again, without resorting to clichés or hard-sell).

Perhaps a case study might be of value to the group.[3] Or you might want to role play a common issue. The point is: help each member of the group get in touch with the way he or she experiences sin. *Christians are not exempt from this process.* The difference between the non-Christian and the Christian is *not* that one sins and the other does not. The only difference is that the Christian has discovered the healing power of Christ. We will never master sin in this life.

Commitment to Christ

The final question in any gospel presentation is how a man or woman, aware of personal need, comes into relationship with Jesus Christ. How does a person become a Christian?

In the Gospel of Mark the answer to this question is spelled out in bold, clear terms.

After John was put in prison, Jesus went into Galilee, proclaiming the good news of God. "The time has come," he said. "The kingdom of God is near. Repent and believe the good news!"

As Jesus walked beside the Sea of Galilee, he saw Simon and his brother Andrew casting a net into the lake, for they were fishermen. "Come, follow me," Jesus said, "and I will make you fishers of men." At once they left their nets and followed him.

When he had gone a little farther, he saw James son of Zebedee and his brother John in a boat, preparing their nets. Without delay he called them, and they left their father Zebedee in the boat with

the hired men and followed him. (Mk 1:14-20)
Note that Mark begins by telling us in general terms about Jesus'
message. Then he describes the specific impact of this preaching in
the lives of four men. Notice the three key elements involved in
coming to Christ: repentance, belief in the gospel and following
Jesus.

Repentance. Freed of its negative connotations of sawdust trails
and weeping penitents, emotion and manipulation, the word simply
means a "change of mind." Specifically, it is used in relationship
to our walk with God. In the Mark 1 passage, Jesus links repentance
with the kingdom of God. He is saying: "Change your mind about
God." Why do we need to change our minds about God and his kingdom? Simply because, as Burton Harding has put it, "we have re-
pudiated the living and true God and have gone into the God-busi-
ness for ourselves. Now we decide to run our lives, choose what we
want, and to make up our own minds about what is right and wrong.
. . . This is basically what the Bible means by sin. It is refusing God
the right to be God in our life. What we generally regard as 'sins'
(stealing, lying, etc.) are simply the signs that we have pushed God
out."[4]

To repent means to change your mind, to decide to no longer live
without God, to let God be the center of your being. We all know that
something is wrong with us. We may not be able to define what is
wrong. We may be totally unaware that our basic problem is our dead
spiritual selves. Yet we do still *experience* the fact that something is
missing. "This separation from God shows up differently with
different people. The disease is the same, the symptoms vary.
Sometimes there is guilt, or lack of meaning in life, or emptiness; at
other times one senses a lack of personal self-control or impure
thoughts."[5] At the core of our being, something is radically wrong—
and we know it. Repentance marks the first step in dealing with this
wrong. It involves an *understanding* of what the wrong is, namely,
a lack of God's presence; a *regret* over what our selfishness has
resulted in; and a *resolve* to become, by God's grace, what we were
meant to be.

Repentance, however, is only the first step. In and of itself, it has no power either to confer forgiveness for the past or to guarantee a better life in the future. If we stop here, we have done nothing more than to make yet another good resolution. This is why our Lord follows the command to repent with the charge to believe the gospel. Repentance indicates our willingness to change. The gospel gives us the power to do so.

Believe the gospel. We are told to "believe the gospel." But what is this *gospel* (literally "good news") that we are to believe? Paul sums it up succinctly.

Now I would remind you, brethren, in what terms I preached to you the gospel, which you received, in which you stand, by which you are saved. . . . For I delivered to you as of first importance what I also received, that Christ died for our sins in accordance with the scriptures, that he was buried, that he was raised on the third day in accordance with the scriptures, and that he appeared to Cephas, then to the twelve. Then he appeared to more than five hundred brethren at one time. (1 Cor 15:1-6 RSV)

The gospel which we are commanded to believe consists of certain facts about Jesus' life—that he died, was buried and then rose again from the dead. To become a Christian we must accept these things to be so. In accepting these facts, we are also accepting Jesus' assessment of himself as the Son of God, because it is by his death and resurrection that we know this to be true.

But there is more to this statement of the gospel than a recitation of historical facts. There are three key words of interpretation—the words *"for our sins."* In the act of repentance we are brought face to face with our real self—the self living in sin, apart from God. We also realize that by ourselves we can do nothing to alter our sin-prone nature or to change our relationship with God. "We cannot straighten or heal ourselves, or create integrity in ourselves, because we have nothing to work with except our sick and disintegrated selves. And since all our fellows share that inherent disability, no other human being can do for us what we cannot do for ourselves. The physician cannot heal himself."[6] To be healed we need outside help. We need

God's help. And this is precisely what we are asked to believe—that Christ has died for sins, and in so doing has dealt with our sinful natures.

But how do we "believe"? What is involved in the act of belief? Certainly there is the idea of intellectual acceptance. No one is capable of consciously following a lie. But when the word *believe* is used in the New Testament, it involves more than mere assent to a set of propositions. If we "believe" in the biblical sense, we act. True belief or faith in certain assertions must issue in action.

Formal belief—intellectual conviction—becomes real belief or faith at the point when we act upon it. When, after considering evidence for and against the proposition that so-and-so is true, we come to a definite conclusion, we have reached formal belief. When our conclusion influences our further thinking and behaviour, we have faith. We not only believe it; we believe in it. We trust it enough to allow it to determine how we live. Real belief is demonstrated in a small but significant way every time we walk across a floor without thinking about what we are doing. We should behave differently if we really believed that what appeared to be a solid floor actually consisted of painted paper laid across an abyss. The Christian, having real belief in a loving God, behaves differently from the person who really believes all notions of God to be convenient but rather juvenile projections of men's current emotional states.[7]

This leads us quite directly to the third and final aspect of becoming a Christian. Once we (1) have understood our true state of alienation from God and have decided to end our rebellion (repentance) and then (2) have come to believe that through Christ's death for our sins this is possible (faith), we are then invited to "follow Christ." Such a step is the inevitable consequence of authentic belief. If we *believe*, we will follow Christ. In the case of the four fishermen, they quite literally followed Jesus, leaving job, family and home to do so.

Follow Christ. No one automatically follows Christ. Each person must choose to do so. Hence following Christ has a beginning point, called conversion. It is the point of turning from sin to Christ. In theological terms, repentance plus faith equals conversion.

It is plain therefore (no matter how much we dislike facing the fact) that every individual is either following Christ or not following Christ. There is no neutral ground. This is, of course, one of the imperatives to evangelism. We look around us and we see the half-lives people are leading and we are compelled to say to them: "There is no reason to go on destroying yourself. Start following Christ. Let him begin to remake you."

We must beware, however, of defining too precisely just when conversion occurs, or what that beginning point must look like. In any study of conversion experiences, the most impressive fact is the variety of responses to Christ. For some, the experience is virtually instantaneous. For others, the turning process is spread over years. For still others, there is never any conscious awareness of the process of turning—only the present consciousness of following Christ.

But the beginning is not the whole story. Notice carefully our Lord's call to Simon and Andrew: "Follow me and *I will make you become fishers of men.*" He is calling them to become something. He wants to make them into something. To follow Christ involves not only beginning but continuing.

The reason for this is clear. When we come to Christ, we are not automatically, instantaneously remade into little saints, full of wisdom and righteousness, perfect in all ways. That part of our nature which is sinful is not eradicated. Rather it is dethroned, taken from the center of our life, and our newly alive spiritual nature becomes the focal point of our personality. But the continuing presence of our old nature signifies warfare. Becoming a Christian marks the beginning of the conflict between our old and new natures—a conflict which is finally resolved only when we meet Christ face to face at death. And only as we continue to follow Christ—as we allow him gradually and patiently to remake us—can we win the battle with sin. Just as we come to Christ, so we follow after him—by repentance and belief. We grow in our understanding and trust of Jesus (belief), and we continue to change our mind about ourselves as we see ourselves ever more clearly and allow our behavior to change (repentance). The Christian life is a life of continuous repentance and faith.[8]

Note too that we are called on to follow a person, not a principle. "Follow *Christ,*" we are told. Quite frankly, one of the problems in the church today is misunderstanding at this point. So often, Christian commitment is conceived of as trust in a creed, loyalty to an institution, or faithfulness in devotion. While all of these are involved in following Christ, they are not the following itself. To be a Christian means to be involved, on the deepest level of our being, with the person of Christ, the Savior who was resurrected and is still alive. To make Christianity less than this is to deny its essence.

This, incidentally, explains how it is possible for conversion experiences to be so different for different people. In conversion, we come to a person *who meets us where we are.* We are not asked to become anything before we can be a Christian. We do not have to clean ourselves up, so to speak. We are asked, simply, to open ourselves, in whatever state we are, to the living Christ who stands outside our life asking entrance.

This also explains why we then begin to grow and change when we come to Jesus. We have entered into a *relationship* with a person and, as in all relationships, we change in response to the ongoing demands the other places on us. If Christianity were mere commitment to a creed, our growth would end at the point when we were able to understand and believe the creed.

Paul Little has summed up commitment to Christ by comparing it to marriage (a comparison sanctioned by Eph 5:21-33).

Mere intellectual assent to facts does not make a person a Christian any more than mere intellectual assent to facts makes a person married. Many people's dissatisfaction with Christianity is because they are like a person who says: "I believe in marriage, I'm sold on marriage, I've read a dozen books on marriage and in the last three months I've been to fifteen weddings, but for some strange reason marriage doesn't mean anything to me." The reason is very simple: he isn't married. Marriage is not a philosophy . . . nor is Christianity . . . rather it is a dynamic relationship with a living person, the Lord Jesus Christ. Just as getting married means giving up our independence, so does receiving Christ. The essence of sin is living independently of God—going my way rather than His way. The essence of repentance is the repudiation of the self-centered principle making Christ and His will the center of my life. When we marry we think of another person in all our decisions. When we receive Christ, we enter into a consultive relationship with Him about every area of our lives.[9]

Such an act of commitment can take place anywhere and anytime. C. S. Lewis was riding a bus when he first opened himself to God. Others have been sitting in a church or standing among inquirers at an evangelistic meeting. John Stott, formerly one of the Queen's Chaplains in England, knelt at his bedside one Sunday night in the dormitory of his public school and told Christ that he had made rather a mess of his life so far; he confessed his sins; he thanked Christ for dying for him; and he asked him to come into his life. The following day he wrote in his diary: "Yesterday really *was* an eventful day! . . . Up till now Christ has been on the circumference and I have but asked Him to guide me instead of giving Him complete control. Behold! He stands at the door and knocks. I have heard Him and now is He come into my house. He has cleansed it and now rules therein."[10]

In chapter 8 I will discuss commitment in the context of a small group. Let me end here with a prayer that might be prayed by a person who has come to the point of commitment.

Lord Jesus, I realize that thus far I have been living my life apart from you, motivated almost solely by what I wanted. I have sinned in thought, word and deed and I am sorry. I now turn from this self-centered life as best I can, and pledge to lead a new life, by your grace, with you as my Master. I believe that this is possible because you died on the cross for my sins. Thank you for what you have done. And now I come to you and commit myself to you. Make of me what you will. I am yours, Lord Jesus, from this day forward. Amen.

Interaction

A Dialog about Commitment

Last week you wrote a dialog in which you and a friend discussed who Jesus is. This week extend the dialog to cover *commitment* to Jesus. Assume that your friend says: "I do believe in Jesus. How do I become his follower?" Try to answer your friend based on Mark 1:14-20 and on the material in this chapter.

Begin by discovering how your friend experiences sin. Help him or her understand (1) what repentance means and (2) what the gospel is—specifically, that Christ died for sin and that commitment to Christ involves active following after him. End by praying a prayer of commitment with your friend.

When you have written these two dialogs (who is Jesus and how a person meets him), continue to run over them in your mind. Imagine other questions being asked and how you would respond. Test various ways of expressing the gospel. These inner dialogs are a valuable way to become comfortable talking about Jesus. They help you think through the issues without consuming great amounts of time.

8
Planning for the Future: The Strategy of Small Group Evangelism

Perhaps it will be by means of small groups meeting in our homes that we will, in fact, reach pagan America. Heaven knows, they don't come to our churches anymore. They aren't at our mass meetings and they certainly don't watch our television evangelists. But they will come in to our homes. Isn't that one of the ways the early church won over pagan Rome?

The training is over. You are now ready to begin outreach. The whole purpose of your small group experience these past weeks is about to be fulfilled. You have been trained to do small group evangelism. Now it is time to get on with that task. In this final chapter I want to discuss the process of planning a multiweek, small group outreach program.

Splitting Up

The basic idea is quite simple. Your training group will split into two or three subgroups, each of which will plan and execute its own small group outreach program. The reason for splitting is that most groups will be too large to be able to add new people. You may well have experienced this problem in your Outreach Event. If you had ten in your training group and each person brought one friend, suddenly you had twenty people. This works for a single event, but not for a multiweek series because you cannot form twenty people into an authentic small group. By definition a small group is not less than five people and not more than thirteen. With less than five, you get informal conversation not small group interaction. With more than thirteen, you get a large group dynamic which becomes leader-centered and is less participatory.

So your training group may have to split. This won't be easy. One small group in Johannesburg faced exactly this problem. They had come together somewhat reluctantly; their pastor had simply appointed each of them to the group, which was to be the church's contribution to a citywide preaching mission. They all showed up, as instructed, but they expected the worst. They survived the first week. The second week was better. The third week they were really enjoying themselves. By the final training session, they had grown so close that they could not bear to dissolve the original group. But being faithful to the purpose of the training, they split the group in half and planned two Outreach Series, each of which sought to reach a different target audience. However, they also agreed to continue meeting at the regular time for prayer and fellowship. I was amazed when I heard this. Here were very busy people willing to give *two* evenings a week to small group activities: one for outreach, the other for fellowship.

I am not suggesting that your group do this. I recall this incident simply to say that it may be very hard to split into outreach groups. But you must resist the temptation to forsake outreach for the sake of fellowship, for groups which turn inward often wither and die. Small groups which survive often have an inward-outward rhythm. In these long-lived groups, at the beginning of their existence together, a lot of time is given over to group building and study. Then, in order to express what they have learned or what they have become, the group takes on a project—raising money for an overseas church, say, or plastering and painting the church foyer, conducting a series of meetings for the high-school group or doing small group evangelism. Then it is back together for another period of regrouping, study and meditation. This inward-outward pattern brings health and vitality to the group.

How you split up will depend on how many are in your group and who you are trying to reach. Typically, a group of twelve would split in two. Each subgroup of six would recruit six non-Christian friends to join the new group. Who goes into which subgroup depends on the target audience to be reached by each. You may decide, for example, that one outreach group will meet in the mornings, while the other would meet in the evening. Four homemakers in the same neighborhood could conduct the morning group; the other subgroup would then run the evening group. In short, decide who you can reach realistically and then divide the group so as to make that possible.

Recruiting New Members
The obvious candidates for invitation to the Outreach Series are people who attended the Outreach Event. They know what is in store for them; they have already met some of the people in the group; and they may have questions which they would like to discuss. They may also know additional people who could be invited; through them you may contact people you would otherwise not reach. So, in order to get the ball rolling, ring up the folks who came to the Outreach Event. Once again, be honest in your invitation. Tell people the plan: The group will meet for six weeks. The first meeting will be exploratory. If after this initial meeting they feel that this group is not for them, they are under no obligation to continue. (In some situations, it may be best to invite your friends to one meeting only and see how that goes. If sufficient interest is expressed at this meeting, you can plan more sessions then and there.) Tell your friends that the overall aim of the group is to discuss the nature and relevance of Christianity, and that the group will be mixed—Christians and non-Christians. The only prerequisite is a desire to learn more about the spiritual aspect of life.

Be upbeat and enthusiastic in your invitations. Remember that you are offering a unique opportunity: the chance to sit down in a comfortable environment with like-minded people and have a serious discussion about a significant topic. Such an opportunity is not to be dismissed lightly, especially today, when watching TV has nearly replaced conversation.

I first learned how hungry people are for real conversation when my wife and I decided to invite some friends for dessert and coffee one evening, asking each person to bring their two favorite poems. We invited more people than we could comfortably seat, since we were sure a lot of people would be "busy." After all, an evening of poetry . . . ? But to our great surprise, everybody we invited came. And they came eagerly. They were excited to read poetry together and talk about it. The evening was a smashing success—we had trouble getting people to leave. We ended around 11:30 P.M., and by midnight most people had got as far as our veranda. The last guest drove off after 12:30 A.M. We later heard that one couple went on talking into the wee hours of the morning.

People are eager to share and to discuss serious topics in an atmosphere of mutual regard and trust. Our topic was poetry, but it could well have been a Bible study of Mark 1. In later years, we did run a weekly Bible study—with the same result. Week after week people came because it was their one opportunity to investigate life-changing issues. Do not sell yourself short by forgetting what a significant opportunity you are creating for your friends.

How many people should you invite? It's hard to say. Experience shows that seventy to eighty per cent of your invitations will be accepted. Remember that you want no more than thirteen people, and that at least thirty per cent but no more than fifty per cent of the group ought to be Christians.

Sometimes a group of Christians will simply not know enough people to invite. You may have to knock on doors in the neighborhood or in the dorm, and invite strangers to your group. This is not a bad idea, for you will meet people who might never otherwise have any contact with Christianity.

If your group decides to visit, I would suggest the following:

1. Set aside an appropriate time to visit. If your aim is to start a morning group for housewives, for example, visit in the morning. Be sure to pick a time when people are likely to be in and not rushed.

2. Meet as a group beforehand to pray and to discuss where you are going to visit. Do not take too much time on this, however, lest you have no time left for visiting!

3. Go out in pairs to visit the predetermined area. At each home: (a) introduce yourself clearly, and say why you have come; (b) chat for a few minutes; (c) leave a written (or printed) invitation giving all the details; (d) if people are interested in attending, consider offering transportation, baby sitters or other help.

Especially when visiting strangers, it is necessary to be quite candid. If you are vague, they may misunderstand the nature of the meeting and feel tricked. Some years ago an energetic group of Christians on one university campus planned a special banquet for athletes. They issued invitations to all the campus athletes, prepared an excellent dinner and invited nationally known sports figures as speakers. They neglected to mention, however, that the banquet was sponsored by a Christian group on campus and that the well-known sports figures were all Christians and would be speaking primarily about their faith and not about sports. A large group of athletes came. But when they discovered what they were attending, they felt they had been tricked. After the banquet, protests were made to university officials, who in turn banned further campus activities of this Christian group. Far from helping evangelism on the campus, the ministry of this group was hindered.

Planning Meetings

Now that you have a group coming to your house, what are you going to do? It is one thing to plan a single Outreach Event, but how do you plan an Outreach *Series*?

Topic. The first consideration is the topic—the topic of the whole series and of each individual meeting. The principle for choosing a

topic for a single Outreach Event applies as well to a series: *Pick a topic that will interest your target group.*
If you are a university student, what are the hot issues on campus? The nuclear freeze? How to get a job in a tight economy? Sexuality? Each of these could be discussed from a Christian point of view in the course of which the gospel could be made quite clear. If you treat something explosive like sexuality or the arms race, however, be sure that you know what you are talking about! You will want to have informed and mature insights to offer. You may need to invite an authority to lead your group.

Rather than taking up a contemporary concern, you might raise a new issue, something your friends may not have thought much about but which they could get interested in. For example, What if Jesus really was God, who became a man? Is there any evidence for this? What difference would it make? These are good questions; a lot of people would like answers to them. And, of course, the topic is ideally suited to an evangelism group.

Or perhaps the topic will emerge from a book chosen for study or a film you watch. C. S. Lewis's *The Problem of Pain,* for example, discusses a topic of interest to many people. The book itself provides the content for group discussion.

Many people are interested in studying the Bible, if only because it is considered "great literature," or because it has been such a decisive influence in Western culture. So you should seriously consider organizing an evangelistic Bible study. By studying one of the Gospels, the people will not only begin to be familiar with the Bible, they will begin to discover Jesus as well.

The church year provides many good topics. During Advent you could do a four-week series on the Incarnation. During Lent the series could be on the death and resurrection of Jesus. Both small group experiences could be climaxed by attending together the festive Christmas or Easter worship service at a local church.

Designing an exciting session. Having the topic is one thing; interacting with it in a meaningful and interesting fashion is another. How does one design a good small group session?

First, decide how your content will be presented. (I have discussed message formats on pp. 78-80). Pick a format that will interest your target group. Make sure, however, that the film (or book or tape) is well done and says the sort of things you feel will provoke good interaction.

Second, design your session around this input. Typically, a session will have three major parts to it: (1) an introduction that will generate interest in the topic and prepare the group for the materials about to be presented, (2) the central presentation and (3) interaction after the materials have been presented. Assign to each part an appropriate amount of time. In a one-hour session, for example, you might decide to have twenty minutes of general group discussion in which people can share experiences related to the topic, twenty minutes to listen to the cassette, and twenty minutes to discuss it.

If you think of the evening session as a series of discrete but interconnected units, each with its own objective, format and content, you will find that the interest level of the group is sustained throughout.

The introduction serves to arouse interest in the topic. Your aim is to give the group a reason for getting involved in the session. You can do this by personalizing the issue (showing how the topic relates to their felt-needs or how it relates to their own experience); by focusing on the topic itself ("This is why you'll enjoy the session . . ."); or by sharing how the topic is of benefit ("Once you understand this, a lot of other things will become clear").

The central presentation is devoted to the input itself. Your aim here is to promote active listening, viewing or discussion. You might give an outline of the presentation so the group will be able to follow it better, or ask several questions for people to keep in mind during the presentation, or alert everyone to watch for certain key features.

The purpose of interaction is to help people understand and apply what has been presented. This could take a variety of forms, including discussion, role play (this is the best way to get a person to identify with an issue) and sharing (helping people relate the material to their life and needs).

Until you gain experience in planning small group sessions, you might want to rely on prepared materials. The small group materials produced by Lyman Coleman (Serendipity House, Box 1012, Littleton, CO 80160) are particularly helpful for transforming a group of strangers into a caring fellowship. A good topic-oriented series is the thirteen-week course prepared by Keith Miller and Bruce Larson called *The Edge of Adventure: An Experiment in Faith* (Word Books). It includes study guides, leaders guides and three cassette tapes. For small group Bible study, I would recommend LifeBuilder Bible Studies (InterVarsity Press). Their discussion questions help you discover and apply the meaning of Old and New Testament books and topics. The Neighborhood Bible Study series (Tyndale) is also recommended. *Creative Ideas for Small Groups in the Christian Community* by John Mallison (Renewal Publications, Box 130, West Ryde, N.S.W. Australia) is very helpful, though it is a difficult book to find. (Some of this material is not evangelistic. You will have to be selective and adapt it to your own needs.)

Developing good questions. There is stimulating discussion and there is boring discussion! And the difference between the two often turns on the quality of the questions asked by the discussion leader. There are various *kinds* of questions; each serves a different purpose in discussion.

Fact questions encourage careful observation. We are all lazy observers. No one person will see everything of significance in a film, for example. Therefore, fact questions often begin with *who, where* or *when,* drawing attention to the people, the place and the time of the materials to be discussed. These questions are easy to answer and so will facilitate wide participation. Fact questions ought not to consume more than fifteen to twenty per cent of the available time, however, for their purpose (apart from getting people to talk) is to lay the groundwork for a discussion about the meaning and the application of the material studied.

Whereas fact questions consider the external and obvious components, *meaning questions* require the group to synthesize observations and grasp the significance of the material. These are more difficult questions to answer, since they require the ability to connect various insights. Often these questions begin with *what, why* or *how. What* questions focus on the events and the interaction of people in a particular setting. *How* questions examine the sequence of actions, seeking to discover cause and effect. *Why* questions are interpretive, forcing people to probe for reasons and explanations.

Application questions move a group from a disinterested consideration of the nature and meaning of the film (or book) to a personal understanding of just how these issues affect their own lives. These questions move a discussion from the realm of the abstract and theoretical into that of the concrete and personal. What was it in the film or book that moved you? amused you? disturbed you? gave you insight into your own situation? You can use these questions to identify points of resonance between the material studied and the life history of each person in the group. Often the key to effective application is the leader's ability to model openness by sharing personal experiences or insights. This frees others to do the same.

In addition to the three basic types of questions (fact, meaning, application), there are other questions which facilitate small group discussion. *Icebreaking questions* provide an opportunity for each participant to declare, This is who I am. These questions ask people to reveal a little bit about who they are: where they live, what they do, and how they got connected with this particular group. Five minutes of such history-giving can release a lot of tension (Who are these other folks? and What are they thinking of me?). It can also diminish the threat that the subjective (and unspoken) needs of individuals will sabotage the stated objectives of the group. These icebreaking questions should not be complex or demanding. You can say, for example, "We'll go around the circle. Each person give your name and tell us how you happen to be here today." In an ongoing small group, of course, such introductions are not necessary, though even here it is wise to begin with some brief personal sharing.

Interaction questions help members of the group to talk to one another. For example, "Harry, do you agree with Sue?" or "John, we haven't heard from you yet. What do you think?" *Generalizing questions* help a group move from specific focused discussion of a particular point into consideration of its wider implications. *Personalizing questions* move in the opposite direction. They take a general discussion and move it into the personal sphere. For example, "How can we, as members of this group, help families in this situation?" *Clarifying questions* seek to introduce other information that might illumine the issue. For example, "Does anyone know anything about this that could help us decide if this is a reasonable solution?" *Critical questions* encourage people to consider both sides by evaluating, pro and con, actions or choices under consideration. For example, "Who will speak in defense of Paul's actions?"

Planning the first session. The first meeting in the Outreach Series is often the most crucial session, because people are deciding then whether they want to continue as part of the group. In this initial session, aim to do two things: create an opportunity for people to get to know one another, and generate interest in the topic itself.

You can build a sense of group identity by asking icebreaking questions. Try to make these questions fit in with the theme of the evening. If you are discussing loneliness, for example, your final icebreaking question might be: "Can you remember as a child ever being lonely?" This allows everyone to talk about themselves, and launches the group in the direction of the topic. (Lyman Coleman is particularly good at this. See his *Encyclopedia of Serendipity*, in which he lists over fifty history-giving exercises and describes sixteen small group sessions, forty-five minutes each, which help to build a group.)

Food helps here too. Be sure to provide space and time to eat together. Sharing a meal or even a cup of coffee draws people together.

The Christians in the group ought to make it their prime responsibility on that first evening to get to know all the new people and make them feel welcome and at ease. Extend to the new people the same love and care that was experienced in the training sessions. In fact, this is the secret to group building. When people enter an atmosphere in which genuine fellowship prevails, they may not be able to define what is going on, but they want to be a part of it.

If you have chosen your topic carefully based on the needs and interests of the group you have invited, generating interest in the topic will be easier. Demonstrate that the topic will be treated with integrity, and that new insights will emerge from the group discussion. Be sure too that the format is appealing. It is a lot more fun watching a film about the topic than listening to a forty-minute lecture. A book is less stimulating than the presence of the author.

So, give it your best shot on the first evening. Your guests will be asking whether it is worth their time to be there. You must prove to them that it will be both fun and profitable.

Calling for commitment. The fifth and final aspect of planning your Outreach Series is the call to commitment to Christ. How does one do this in the context of a small group? Won't people be embarrassed or offended? No, provided the call to commitment is genuine, not manipulative, and fits the context and the ethos of the group.

There are several ways to encourage people to commit their lives to Christ. In the meeting itself, you might pray a prayer of commitment at the final session in the series and encourage those who are ready to follow Christ to repeat it silently after you. This will be appropriate, if you have been ending each group meeting in prayer anyway, and if, a week or so prior to this, you have said to the group, "At our final meeting I am going to take the liberty of concluding by praying what is called 'a prayer of commitment.' I want to do this because I know some of you have been weighing the alternatives and might be ready then to commit your lives to Christ. Others of you may not yet be ready to do that, but that too is O.K." This procedure gives group members time to think about this act of commitment well beforehand, and they will not be surprised by it at the last meeting. You might even want to end your Outreach Series with a brief, liturgical worship service. You can print up an "Order of Worship" with responsive readings, songs and a prayer of commitment.

In other groups, commitment will come in the context of personal conversation. This is one reason it is important for each Christian to learn what is involved in talking about commitment. Perhaps you will have the joy of seeing a friend come to Christ during the coffee time after a small group session, the next day at lunch or while out walking together.

Still other groups may want to link their activities into a larger evangelistic effort. Rather than calling for commitment in the context of the small group meeting itself, the whole group might attend a worship service at which the speaker gives an invitation to follow Christ. Or the group might go to a special series of evangelistic meetings sponsored by a church or campus fellowship, praying that non-Christians will decide to follow Christ in that context. How commitment is urged is not important; that people are given a clear opportunity to decide for Christ, is.

The training course is now at an end. I hope that it has been a rich experience for you and that it has provided adequate training to enable you to begin sharing the good news about Jesus with your friends—on both an individual and a group level. As you begin to put this training into practice, remember what H. R. Weber said about the early Christians: "One of the clues to the spontaneous mission of the ancient Church was the *strong consciousness of being God's own peculiar people.*"[1] Herein lies the secret to our motivation: an awareness of our calling to be God's people in this world; to be the salt of the world and the light in a darkened age. As Peter put it: "You are a chosen race, a royal priesthood, a holy nation, *God's own people,* that you may declare the wonderful deeds of him who called you out of darkness into his marvelous light" (1 Pet 2:9 RSV).

At the same time we must avoid being overwhelmed by what Douglas Hyde has called a "minority complex."

From the time I joined the Communist Party, practically to the time when 24 years later I left it, I was conscious of the fact that our members firmly believed that, relatively few though they might be, they had a world to win and were going to win it. I came to the Catholic Church prepared for most of what I found—and it would be sheer hypocrisy to pretend that I either expected or found everything to be good. But one thing I had not bargained for was the many people I met who told me that the Catholic community in Britain suffered from something they described as a minority complex. I had not expected this, because I was coming from an organization which at that time had some 45,000 members to one which was numerically 100 times as strong and which represented some 10 percent of Britain's population.

Even in the days when we Communists could only boast some 15,000 members, we believed that when the right circumstances came, as come they must, we would make Britain Communist and would do so with the support of the mass of the people. Whatever else we may have suffered from, we had no minority complex.

Coming straight, as it were, from one world to another, it astounded me that there should be people with such numbers at their disposal, and with the truth on their side, going around weighed down by the thought that they were a small beleagured minority carrying on some sort of an impossible fight against a big majority. The very concept was wrong. Psychologically it was calamitous. And there was nothing in the facts, so far as I could see, to warrant such an approach.[2]

Let us flee from this "minority complex," simply because it is a lie. We are not "a beleaguered minority carrying on . . . an impossible fight." We are God's own people, followers of the risen Christ—the Christ who has defeated all powers (Col 1:16; 2:15). Even though it may appear that evil rules on this earth now, the reality is that Christ reigns. And one day, in the fullness of time, that reign will be known to all. As it is now, we as Christians are called on to spearhead the spread of the kingdom of God here on earth. Let us joyfully accept this calling, as we trust in the reality of Christ's presence and power.

Rest on our Lord's words to you: "You did not choose me, but I chose you and appointed you that you should go and bear fruit" (Jn 15:16 RSV).

Interaction
What Next?
This exercise has two purposes: to serve as a review of the past and to stimulate planning for the future. Both are essential parts of strategy. Both are necessary if you are going to translate your convictions into action. Both are necessary if this course

is to be of any practical value.

1. What are the major lessons you have learned in the past weeks?

2. How have you begun to put these ideas into practice?

3. What insights and skills do you think will be of use to you in the future?

4. What ideas are still unclear to you?

5. What can you do to gain further insight?

6. What does the phrase "to witness is to be honest" now mean to you? In what ways have you become a more honest person?

7. Who have you been praying for and what has happened so far? What must you continue to pray about?

8. Have you become friends with more non-Christians in the past weeks?

9. What have your attempts at verbal witness been like? What has or has not happened?

10. What friends can you invite to the Outreach Series?

11. What can you do in a practical way to ensure that they are able to attend?

12. How have you become newly *aware* of opportunities for witness—by word and

by deed?

13. Could you carry on an intelligent conversation about who Jesus is and how a person can know him?

14. If not, what are your plans for developing this art?

15. Most important of all, is Jesus more real to you now?

Part 2
The Experience:
A Training Series
for Small Groups

To learn *about* small group evangelism, you need only read Part 1 of *Small Group Evangelism*. All the key ideas are there. To learn *how to do* small group evangelism, it is necessary to be a part of a small training group. The materials in Part 2 are designed to guide such a training group. Following these step by step will help you grasp the ideas in Part 1 and transform them into actual small group outreach.

Between small group sessions you will need to do some preparation work. The Homework section at the end of each set of small group exercises will specify what is necessary. Your preparation work will usually involve *reading* the next chapter, *writing* out responses to the interaction exercises, and *acting* on the material you have studied.

Session 1
The Principles of Evangelism

A. Leader's Introduction (10 min.)

Discuss the aims for this training group, its schedule and the obligations for each member. (Build on the information listed below.)

1. The *aim* of this training group: to learn the ideas and skills necessary to do small group evangelism; to develop the kind of warm, caring small group that will facilitate such outreach.

2. The *schedule* for the group: nine sessions—eight training sessions and an Outreach Event.

3. The *obligations* of group members: to read one chapter of *Small Group Evangelism* per week and do the interaction exercises; to participate actively in the small group by attending each session and joining in the exercises.

B. Getting to Know One Another (20 min.)

Beginning with the leader, go around the group giving your name and then taking about a minute to answer the first question. Go around the circle a second time and each answer question two. The third question is voluntary (don't go around the circle a third time).

1. What do you do or what are you studying? Where do you live?

Where do you come from? What is your family background?

2. What do you enjoy doing (for example, sports, hobbies, reading, work, traveling and so on)?

3. When, if ever, did "God" become more than a word to you? (Even though it is optional, take this opportunity to share. It will help the group to know a bit about the real you, as well as giving you the chance to try to put into words your own experience of God.)

C. The Three Principles of Evangelism (30 min.)

Based on the Interaction questions in chapter 1, discuss your answers to the following questions.

1. What is the essence of the Great Commission? What is the difficulty in fulfilling it?

2. What are the three principles of evangelism?

3. What do you think about the idea that "every member is a minister"? What experience of ministry have you had? with what result? What experiences of evangelism?

4. What do you think about the concept of "spiritual gifts"? Which gift(s) do you think you have?

5. What is the role of God in evangelism? What experiences of prayer have you had in relationship to ministry?

6. Take a few minutes to pray for the group, what God can teach you through this training experience, and for those you want to reach with the gospel.

D. My Hopes and Fears about Evangelism (30 min.)

1. What are your hesitations about evangelism?

2. What do you fear might frustrate our efforts in this group?

3. How can we overcome these potential problems?

4. What do you hope might happen as a result of the small group experience?

Homework

1. Read chapter 2 and prepare the interaction exercises.

2. Do the following exercise: Building a Training Group—one way

to put into action these principles of evangelism is by recruiting others to join your training group. Or, if your group already has twelve members, perhaps another training group could be organized for interested friends. The more Christians involved, the wider the gospel can be spread.

1. *Contact* Christian friends from your area and invite them to join a Training Group. Share what you have already learned. Keep at it, until you find at least one new person willing to join the group.

2. *Deliver* a copy of *Small Group Evangelism,* as soon as possible, to those who have agreed to come with you to the group, so that they can catch up. No one will be able to join your group after the second meeting, since it is difficult to develop or maintain a sense of group cohesion if new people are always coming into the group. If additional people are interested in joining your group after week two, start up a new group for them.

3. *Arrange* to accompany your friend to the group, so that she or he will not feel ill at ease entering into a new situation.

4. *Learn* from your act of invitation. Some will say no, others yes. Both are valuable experiences from which to learn and will stand you in good stead later on when you invite other friends to the Outreach Event. Next week, you will have the chance to discuss with the group your experience of trying to invite others.

Session 2
The Problems in Witnessing

A. The Art of Invitation (30 min.)

Last week, each person sought to invite at least one Christian friend to join the training group. Hence, in this session, you either invited someone or were invited. Introduce those you invited and share one interesting fact about each person. If you were invited, when you are introduced, share your first reaction when you were invited to join the group.

After everyone is introduced, look over the questions below, making notes if you like. These questions will serve as the basis for the group discussion.

If you invited others:

1. What success did you have?

2 How did you go about inviting people?

3. What reasons did people give for wanting to join the group? for not joining?

4. What problems had to be overcome before people were free to join?

5. Did you enjoy inviting others? Explain.

6. What did you learn about your own and others' motives?

If you were invited:
1. What was it about this small group that interested you?
2. What made you decide to come?
3. Were there any factors which almost prevented you from coming?
4. What did you like about the way your friend invited you?

B. Witnessing and Me (20 min.)
Turn to the "Witnessing and Me" interaction exercise (pp. 52-53). This will serve as the basis for group discussion.
1. Beginning with the leader, each share briefly (in one minute or less) a particular problem which you face in witnessing.
2. Now begin to discuss how to overcome these various problems.

C. The Witnessing Community (40 min.)
In Acts 4:23-35 we catch a glimpse of the early church. It is an intriguing portrait, well worth careful study; for in this incident we find exactly what we need to launch into small group evangelism: *the model of what a witnessing community is like.*

The whole chain of events begins when Peter heals a crippled beggar at the Temple gate (Acts 3:1-10). Then in a sermon he points out that the source of this healing power is Jesus who was crucified but is now alive again (3:11-26). The religious officials do not like this at all (they killed Jesus), and so they arrest and jail Peter and his companion John (4:1-17). Peter and John are released the next day but are commanded "not to speak or teach at all in the name of Jesus" (4:18), an order which they bluntly refuse to obey. In Acts 4:23-35, we meet them as they return to the group of believers.

After reading the passage, take eight to ten minutes to answer the following questions:
1. Go back over this passage and make a list of *the characteristics of the group.* What was the group like?
2. Now list the different factors that *motivated* this group to witness.
3. From the characteristics and motivation of this first-century

church, what can we learn of value for the church today? for this group?

4. Based on the covenant on p. 54 in the interaction exercise, prepare a group covenant and commit it to God in prayer.

Homework

1. Read chapter 3 and prepare the interaction materials.

2. If possible, obtain and read the booklet *Tyranny of the Urgent* by Charles Hummel (InterVarsity Press). The author discusses the problem of time and our seeming lack of it.

3. Pick one particular problem which you feel is hindering your own witness and consciously work on it this week. If your problem is, say, that you just cannot believe all your friends need Christ, you can meet this by (1) praying that God will give you insight into the real needs of people, (2) reading Scripture to see what it has to say and (3) perhaps discussing your feelings with a Christian friend.

Whatever the problem, discuss it with someone else in the group and go over your plans to overcome it.

Session 3
The Skills of
a Christian
Conversationalist

A. The Christian Conversationalist (10 min.)
In preparation for the discussion, spend the first few minutes together reflecting on the content of chapter 3. What is a Christian conversationalist?

B. Sharing Exercise (30 min.)
Christian conversation involves the ability to share informally what is happening in our lives *because we are Christians*. How would you respond, honestly and as a Christian, to each of the following three situations? Make notes if necessary. After five minutes, you will have a chance to discuss your responses with the group.

1. Over a cup of coffee, a friend says to you, "What is that small group all about? You know, the one you go to each week?" You answer . . .

2. Your neighbor greets you as you return from church. You start chatting and eventually he asks: "You're strange, you know, all the time you spend at church. Why do you bother to go? Nobody else goes anymore." You answer . . .

3. You discover that one of the men in the neighborhood is out

of work. He and his wife have three small children. Neither can find work; they are struggling to make ends meet. You *act* as a Christian by . . .

After five to seven minutes, have one or two people read their responses to question 1. Discuss these. Do the same for questions 2 and 3. Are the responses all they could be? Are the answers accurate? Are they interesting or intriguing? (We should not bore people when discussing Christianity!) Are the responses free of Christian jargon? (That is, will the other person understand what is being said?)

C. The Art of Listening (20 min.)
The following is an exercise in listening. The group will divide into pairs. Each pair will then discuss a controversial subject. One person will argue vigorously one side of the issue; the other person must reply with an opposing view. It does not matter what your true feelings on the subject may be, since this is only an exercise.

The only rule guiding the argument is that before you can respond, you must summarize in your own words the point which your partner has made. Only when your partner agrees that an accurate summary has been given, can you go on and make your own point.

For example, if the controversial subject is: "Football is a bad sport for youth," Harry might say "I think football is bad because it brings out the worst passions. Fellows try to hurt one another and they break rules when the referee is not looking." Summarizing, Michael replies, "You're saying that football is bad because people lose their tempers and hurt one another and try to take unfair advantage of the other team." Harry nods agreement, so Michael goes on to make his own point: "But I think that though this sometimes happens, the exercise toughens our youth and the teamwork teaches them the value of cooperation."

"So you're saying," Harry rejoins, "that any violence is outweighed by the good done to the physique and by the value of learning to cooperate with team members, but I say . . ." And so on. Your group leader may want to *demonstrate* with a volunteer how to do this reflecting-back exercise.

The following are examples of controversial subjects you may wish to argue about:

1. Professional sports should be banned.
2. Abortion should be outlawed.
3. The U.S.A. should give up its nuclear weapons stockpile.
4. Women ought not to be allowed to become ministers.
5. Marriage is passé.
6. This is an awful university (city, church).

The point is *not* to seek consensus and insight into these issues. The issues are secondary. The point is to find topics that will create heated discussion and thus point out how hard it is to listen!

Now find a partner and argue! After five minutes, come back together and discuss for the next ten minutes what you have learned.

D. Problem-Solving (30 min.)
We witness by words and deeds. When a friend is facing a problem, we use words to help our friend find direction at a difficult time, and by our deeds we demonstrate how Christ can help us live life.

Our aim in such situations is not to give advice as experts (which we probably are not anyway), but to help our friend discover what the problem is and what options are open. Then a sensible decision can be made.

The process of solving problems has four parts to it:

1. *What are the facts of the situation?* This may be the point at which you are of most help to a troubled friend. By asking questions and then pinpointing each of the relevant factors, your friend is helped to sort through what appeared to be a confusing situation.

2. *What is the real issue?* While talking through the problem, it usually becomes clearer just what the core issue is, about which a decision must be made. We often feel overwhelmed by a problem because we have failed to specify what it is that we must face.

3. *What decision must be made?* Your friend must decide between options. Your friend must do this. Resist the temptation to decide for her or him; for if you do, in a subtle way you become responsible for the outcome of the decision and your friend will lack commitment

to carry it through.

4. *What plans are necessary to carry out the decision?* It is one thing to decide, it is quite another to do. Help your friend plan the steps necessary to put into practice the decision taken. Be very specific. Assign time and place when and where certain things are to be done.

Your role is to ask questions (remember the value of reflecting-back responses), to listen carefully (and so pinpoint what really is being said), and then to ask more questions. Be careful not to argue, interrupt, pass judgment, jump to conclusions or be shocked or annoyed.

Your group leader may now *demonstrate,* by role play, how such a problem-solving conversation might flow. Or you may immediately split into threes. Each of you decide which problem you want to discuss. It is best if this is a real problem but an imagined one may work as well.

Once each of you has chosen a problem, the exercise proceeds as follows:

First Run: Person No. 1 tries to help No. 2 with his problem (which No. 2 will state) while No. 3 acts as an observer. After five minutes the exercise will be stopped and there will be three minutes for discussion. The observer (No. 3) first gives his evaluation, then the consultant (No. 1) says how far he felt he made progress and the consultee (No. 2) says how he felt. Then general discussion follows (within the triads) *not* about details of the problem involved but about the effectiveness of the consultation. The observer should note points like: Did the helper monopolize the conversation or not? Was he a good listener? Was he judgmental? Did he give too much advice? Did he argue for his own point of view? Did he help the other to see the issues better or, if they got that far, come to a decision about the next step?

Second Run: The procedure is repeated with No. 2 helping No. 3 with the problem and No. 1 observing.

Third Run: As above, with No. 3 helping No. 1 and No. 2 observing.

Feedback: The whole group will then discuss what they felt about the exercise and what they learned.[1]

Homework

1. Read chapter 4 and prepare the interaction materials.

2. If possible, locate and read John White's "Is Witnessing Brainwashing?" (chapter 9 in *The Race*, InterVarsity Press, 1984).

3. Make a list of people about whom you can pray and with whom you can seek to share your faith.

4. Try out in a deliberate fashion each of the conversational skills discussed and practiced in this session. *Sharing:* think about typical questions which interested non-Christian friends might ask you and rehearse in your mind how you could answer clearly and honestly. *Listening:* exercise your listening skills; concentrate all your attention on what he or she is saying and from time to time reflect back what is said to you. Afterward discuss this attempt with the person. *Problem-solving:* be alert to problems in your life and the lives of others to which you can apply your skills.

Session 4
The Process of Planning

A. Group Prayer (30 min.)

A group that is not praying for *specific* people will usually not reach *any* people for Christ. It really is that simple. If we are not concerned enough to pray, we won't be concerned enough to witness. The purpose of this exercise, therefore, is to focus on prayer. As you pray together, remember the words of our Lord: "Where two or three come together in my name, there am I with them" (Mt 18:20). As you pray, Jesus is present!

Pray together in a conversational fashion. That is, each individual prays briefly about one topic at a time; others pray about that same topic; when that topic has been prayed about, move to a new (though related) topic. In other words, each of you will pray several brief prayers rather than one long prayer. If this idea of conversational prayer is new to you, keep the following suggestions in mind:

□ *Pray in the first person* when you are referring to yourself. This is the only way to real honesty in prayer. Instead of "Lord, we ought to pray more often, and we ought to read our Bibles more often, forgive us," pray, "Lord, forgive me. I've read my Bible only once or twice this week, and I've just prayed on-the-run, and my heart is so hungry to be with you alone. Please forgive me for this, and I put the control of my day back into your hands." When praying on behalf of the whole group, "we" is appropriate.

☐ *Pray specifically*—not, "Lord, help me to speak more boldly," but "Lord, give me a natural opportunity next week to speak to Carol about you."

☐ *Pray simply.* Speak to God as you would to a friend. Share with him what you are really feeling. There is no need to construct elaborate sentences filled with lofty theological phrases.

☐ *Pray in ordinary English.* There is no need to use "Thee" and "Thou" when addressing God.

☐ *Pray in a loud enough voice* so that others can hear you easily and thus pray along with you.

Begin by sharing briefly your experience of trying to be a "Christian conversationalist" during the past week. What worked out well? What went wrong? Were you afraid even to try? Pray together about these experiences (10 minutes).

During the time remaining, let each person share the names of one or two people who might be invited to an Outreach Event. Share briefly who they are and what their relationship to Christianity is. Pray together about each of these people.

B. Planning an Outreach Event (1 hour)
You have read about how to plan a small group Outreach Event. In the next hour you will actually plan one. The idea is this. Between training sessions 5 and 6, your group will plan and execute an Outreach Event to which you will invite your friends. In this way you will learn far more about small group evangelism than you could ever learn just from a book. Furthermore, it is easier and less threatening to plan a single event, than it is to launch straight into planning a seven-week series.

First, *the ideas.* Your small group leader will review with you the process of planning a small group Outreach Event.

Second, the *target group.* Who will you invite?

Third, *content.* What topic would interest your target group and how will you approach it?

Fourth, *place/time/structure*. When and where will you hold the meeting? What food is appropriate? What will be the format for the meeting?

Fifth, *organization:* Who will arrange for each aspect of the evening?

In order to answer these questions creatively, I suggest that you try "brainstorming" together. Brainstorming is a group technique often used by business and industry to free up their executives to explore new avenues of growth and development. It works like this. A topic is set before a group. (In this case: To what aspect of the gospel will our target group best respond and how can we put together a creative evening around it?) Then people are asked to make suggestions as quickly as possible without regard to whether the ideas are feasible or not. All suggestions will be recorded. Outlandish ideas are welcomed (they often trigger other ideas). No criticism is allowed. This is important. It is the fear of suggesting a "dumb idea" that often inhibits our creativity in a group. Finally, after a sufficient period of time, stop brainstorming and go back over the list and look for the best idea. You will be amazed at how creative you have been.

Homework

1. Read chapter 5 and prepare the interaction materials.

2. Think and pray about which friends you could invite to the Outreach Event (on the basis of the group decision as to the target group).

3. Invite these friends to the Outreach Event. Be sure to be open about what has been planned. Do not be apprehensive. If the group has done a good job in planning (as I am sure it has), the event will be fun, relaxed and highly profitable.

4. Pray for these friends, for the Outreach Event, for each group member, for yourself.

5. Continue to be open to getting to know more non-Christians.

Session 5
The
Interactions of
a Small Group

A. Group Prayer (15 min.)
Once again, begin your small group experience by praying together. Pray conversationally. Pray for each other. Pray especially for the Outreach Event.

B. Group Process (1 hour)
You have read about small group dynamics. Now it is time to analyze how your own group functions and to assess each individual's role in the group.

1. Review quickly the key points in chapter 5 (10 min.). Make sure you understand (a) the difference between the objective side and the subjective side of group functioning, (b) the ways group tension can be dealt with, (c) the variety of ways people interact in a small group, and (d) the vision of becoming an honest, accepting and loving fellowship.

2. Complete the questionnaire "The Small Group and Me" (p. 96) if you have not already done so.

3. What role description best describes how you generally function in a group? The leader will begin this discussion by sharing her or

his favorite role. Does anyone else in the group also play this role? What are the benefits of each role? the dangers? After the discussion of roles, discuss what you have learned in general about how groups function.

4. Spend the last ten minutes discussing the Outreach Event. Who might be coming? What role(s) are they likely to play in the group? How can we help them feel comfortable and part of the group?

C. Group Planning (15 min.)
Review your plans for the Outreach Event. Have all the details necessary to make it run smoothly been attended to?

Homework
1. Insofar as you are able, repair any strained relationships in your small group. These may have become apparent as you worked on "The Small Group and Me" exercise. Do this before the Outreach Event if possible.

2. Fulfill your responsibility for the Outreach Event and participate actively in the project. Pray for the event, especially for those who will be attending.

3. Read chapter 6 and prepare the interaction materials.

Session 6
The Content of Our Witness (I)

This past week you had your first experience of small group evangelism. I hope this was a really good experience for you—so much so that you are now feeling more excited than ever to get on with the whole outreach program. However, I know that for most people this first experience had its moments of personal trauma. Our emotions are funny things, especially when we go into any new experience. Hence I think it would be of value, before getting into the group exercises for session 6, to look briefly at some of these feelings to see what they really mean and what we can learn from them.

Apprehension. I suspect that one feeling most people had when they were planning the outreach group was apprehension. We generally *fear* any new situation. The reason for this is simple enough—because the situation is new we cannot anticipate what will happen. When we cannot anticipate, then we begin to *imagine* all that could go wrong.

In all this remember that such fears are quite natural. The important thing is not to give in to our fears by retreating from the fearful situation.

Second, many of our fears are based on wrong assumptions. For example, we fear no one will be interested in Christianity. But this is not so. In my work I have found exactly the opposite. Most people are deeply interested in Christianity as long as they are not bludgeoned into listening or otherwise manipulated.

Third, whatever happens can be made into a good and profitable experience. When no one showed up for one small group, they used the time to ask *why* no one came. This resulted in a most profitable discussion. They recognized certain mistakes they had made. Then they went on to make better plans for the next attempt. Finally, they prayed together for the next meeting, which was highly successful. Often we let the "failure" discourage us: "Oh, well, I knew it wouldn't work." And we never try again.

Fourth, we become apprehensive when we fail to rely on God. He has called us to such outreach attempts and hence he is with us in our every effort and will use whatever happens.

Discouragement. If apprehension is the emotion that assails us before the event, then discouragement is our enemy afterward. *Discouragement comes when what happens falls short of or is different from what we expected.* We expect six couples and only four actually come. So we have failed. Or during the discussion only one or two people seem to have understood the point of the tape recording. Hence, we feel that we have failed.

But is this "failure"? Hardly. All it really says is that we can never know beforehand just what will take place.

Remember, first, that numbers are not an infallible measure of success. A meeting of two thousand is not necessarily a more significant meeting than one of five people. Second, do not measure success or failure on the basis of your own interpretation. The problem may be that your anticipation was faulty. Third, get rid of the success/failure mentality altogether! In God's eyes the question is: Have you done the best you could? Fourth, remember that you seldom know what is happening within another person. At times the least expected things make the deepest impact upon others. After all, it is the Holy Spirit who is working in them in his own way. Finally, *learn* from your real mistakes (you will make some). Do not let them discourage you. Mistakes are not tragedies, they are opportunities for learning.

Unexpected difficulties. There is yet another factor to be taken into account. If your group has the potential to make a real impact on others, you must anticipate unexpected difficulties. I say this because of a pattern which I have seen emerge around the ministry of a group of which I was a part for years. Every time we were about to launch a new outreach effort, problems crowded in upon us. Our relationships with one another became problematic; or we all experienced unusual and uncharacteristic depression; or we were called to help in a crisis in someone's life which sapped time and energy.

I noticed this same sort of phenomenon at several university missions we conducted. In each, just when things were going well, the executive committee began to fall apart. In two cases, key committee members were hauled before their faculty advisors and told to drop immediately all outside activities as they were in danger of failing. (Both had previously received A's, and both did ultimately pass very easily.) The week before the main lecture series on one campus, despite an excellent response to early mission activities, the whole committee was depressed. Other things had crowded in—boyfriend trouble, family crises, and so on.

Problems are part of living—but why the sudden flood, affecting so many people, at such a crucial time? I feel the answer is wrapped up in Paul's assertion that ". . . we are not contending against flesh and blood, but against the principalities, against the powers, against the world rulers of this present darkness, against the spiritual hosts of wickedness in the heavenly places" (Eph 6:12 RSV). As Christians we take the supernatural seriously—both the divine and the demonic. We believe that this world is in the grip of the dark powers. Hence, we expect to face demonic opposition if we start to rock the devil's boat and actually win others to Jesus Christ. As C. S. Lewis has put it, "There is no neutral ground in the universe; every square inch, every split second, is claimed by God and counterclaimed by Satan."[2]

We need to go into outreach groups with an awareness, born

through prayer, of God's presence and of his victorious power. Incidentally, in no situation have such unanticipated problems actually ruined an effort. They just made the going tougher.

Success. A word is in order for those of you who had no fear, no discouragement, no particular problems. You had a superb time during your Outreach Event. I suspect that as you keep on in your outreach efforts you will face some of what I have mentioned. But for the time being, just file this section away for future reference.

A. Evaluating the Outreach Event (30 min.)

Discuss your Outreach Event on the basis of your responses to the questionnaire in the Interaction on pp. 108-9.

B. Who Jesus Is (1 hour)

This will be an exercise in trying to say clearly and concisely just who Jesus is based on your reading of chapter 6 and your work on "A Dialog about Jesus" (p. 110). Split into subgroups of three. In each triad, one member will be the "Christian," a second is the "interested non-Christian," while the third is the "observer."

The Christian then will try to explain to the non-Christian who Jesus is. The non-Christian is not an antagonist asking difficult or peripheral questions but a genuinely interested person. The questions ought to reflect this. The ᶦob of the non-Christian is to get the Christian to speak clearly and unambiguously. During the dialog, the observer will be making notes: Is the explanation clear? accurate? to the point? free of jargon? When the dialog is complete, the observer will lead a discussion of its effectiveness.

During the first run, the non-Christian will begin by asking, "Tell me, who is Jesus?" The Christian will seek to explain without discussing the work of Jesus. In other words, concentrate on the first point of the outline given in chapter 6.

In run two, the Christian will seek to communicate what Jesus *did.* In run three the Christian will explain what the work of Christ means to the individual. Therefore, each role play is different; each starting where the last left off. This exercise may prove difficult at first. Do not be overly frustrated if you find yourself hard put as the Christian to express what you mean. Rather, allow this frustration to lead you to more study and practice.

After everyone has had the opportunity to play each of the three roles, use the remaining time to reflect as a whole group on this experience of trying to share who Jesus is.

Homework

1. Read chapter 7 and prepare the interaction materials.

2. Pray about an opportunity to discuss who Jesus is with someone this week. The dialog you have written and the role play you did have prepared you for this. Be sensitive to situations. It is best, of course, to discuss who Jesus is with someone seeking this answer. But it may be that you will have to do this with your spouse or a Christian friend. This is all right. You will still gain experience and confidence. A man I know tried this exercise with his Bible study group and discovered that one member was desperately seeking the answer to this very question—who *is* Jesus?

3. Pray for those who attended the Outreach Event. What is your further responsibility to them? How can you follow up their interests, or their needs?

4. Follow up these friends.

Session 7
The Content
of Our
Witness (II)

A. Spiritual Pilgrimage (45 min.)

How did you come to know Christ? Each person's story is different; and each illustrates how God works in a life. In chapters 6 and 7 the focus was on the objective facts of the gospel. In this exercise you will first recall the subjective experience of these facts, and then draw a chart that illustrates the ups and downs of your spiritual pilgrimage (10-15 min.).

Begin by dividing your life into significant time periods. Perhaps they correspond to your *educational experience:* preschool, elementary school, junior high, high school, college, career. Or it may be that *age* is the key factor for you: childhood, adolescence, young adult, young married. For some it is *place* that is crucial: Detroit, Minneapolis, Los Angeles, Iowa farm. Or important people: parents, neighborhood gang, Wendy, Rev. Harrison, Grandfather. Or a combination of factors: childhood, high school, college, Denver.

For each time frame ask: What was the level of my spiritual awareness then, and what crucial spiritual experiences did I have? In particular, recall your conversion: was this a dramatic event? or did you gradually become aware that you trusted Christ? However this occurred (or is even now occurring), express it as clearly as possible.

Combine these two factors into a chart (as illustrated below) in which you sketch your own experience. In groups of three, share your sketches with one another. If there is enough time, tell how you came to know Christ.

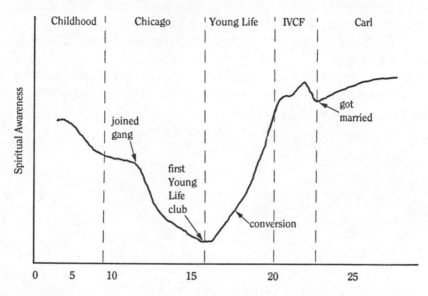

In the final fifteen minutes of this phase, as a whole group discuss ways of telling others about God's actions in our lives. What communicates best? What puts people off? How can such "testimonies" become harmful? helpful? How can we balance the objective and the subjective sides of the gospel?

B. Becoming a Christian (45 min.)

In the same groups of three, do dialogs as you did last week between an "interested non-Christian" and a "Christian," the third person acting as an observer. The question posed by the non-Christian is: "How can I become a Christian?"

Each time someone plays the non-Christian, do so with a problem—drug addiction, loneliness, stress, anxiety, breakdown of a key relationship—or objection of an actual non-Christian friend in mind. Try to hear the gospel through the needs of that friend.

Homework

1. Read chapter 8 and prepare the interaction materials.

2. Continue to share about Christ with your friends. With at least one other person, share your experience of meeting Jesus.

3. Continue to pray for such opportunities, for yourself as well as for your friends.

4. By means of an inner dialog, practice explaining how to become a Christian. Imagine discussing Christ with a friend. What would he or she say? How would you respond?

Session 8
The Strategy of Small Group Evangelism

A. Past and Future (30 min.)
On the basis of the interaction exercise "What Next?" (pp. 139-42), discuss what you learned in this course and how you plan to use it.

B. Outreach Series (30 min.)
If your group has eight or more members, decide together how you will split up. In two or three subgroups, discuss *who* you will seek to reach, *when* and *how*. Set a time and place for a long meeting to plan this Outreach Series.

C. Worship and Praise (30 min.)
End your training experience with a time of prayer, praise, singing and sharing. Make this a Quaker-style service with each person suggesting a hymn, praying a prayer, giving a word of thanks or praise, recounting moments of significance these past weeks, or reading a few verses of Scripture.

Conclude by sitting or standing in a circle; hold hands and sing the Doxology. Then hug each other!

Part 3
Leader's Guide
for the
Training Group

Part 3 is designed for the leader of the small group training session. It provides all the background material the group leader needs to prepare for a small group session. The actual step-by-step guide for the small group session is in Part 2. It should not be necessary to refer to Part 3 during the small group meeting.

Session 1: The Principles of Evangelism

Aims

1. To begin the group-building process by creating the opportunity for each person to share some of his or her own history.
2. To introduce the concept of small group evangelism and the nature of the training experience.
3. To communicate the Great Commission and the three principles for fulfilling it both on a cognitive and an experiential level.
4. To forge group goals by sharing hopes and fears about the training group and about small group evangelism.

Outline

A. Leader Introduction (10 min.)
B. Getting to Know One Another (20 min.)
C. The Three Principles of Evangelism (30 min.)
D. My Hopes and Fears about Evangelism (30 min.)

B. Getting to Know One Another (20 min.)

It will always be your responsibility as leader to be the first to answer any sharing questions such as these. You are the model. Set an example of brevity and clarity in your answers. Everyone will follow your lead. The aim of this first exercise is not only to help people feel comfortable together as a group, but also to demonstrate that the group will be *participatory* and will discuss spiritual realities. Watch the time carefully in section B. It is very easy to run over in this type of sharing exercise.

You will not have time for everyone to answer question 3. Regulate the number of responses you allow according to the time remaining for section B. You may want to provide time at the beginning of session 2 for other members of the group to tell how God became real to them. (If you feel that question 3 will make the group uncomfortable, ask instead, "When and how did you become involved in the life of the church?")

C. The Three Principles of Evangelism (30 min.)

In section C your aim is to make sure that people grasp (a) the nature of the Great Commission and how it can be fulfilled and (b) the excitement of the challenge all this poses to the Christian. Use the questions to probe people's ideas and feelings about each principle. The pattern of moving from ideas to feelings and experiences is a good one for any group discussion. Pinpoint the key ideas and give people opportunity to tell how they feel about them or to share experiences which affirm their validity.

If the group has not had the opportunity to read chapter 1, you will have to answer the "idea" questions in the form of brief summaries of the contents of the book. Then you can ask the feeling and experience questions.

D. My Hopes and Fears about Evangelism (30 min.)
Here your aim is to get people to express both their hesitations about doing evangelism as well as their aspirations for what could happen if they actually do small group evangelism. The first two questions will allow the group to identify fears they have about being a part of the group and about evangelism in general. Allow these questions only five to seven minutes. Next week you will come back to the question of fears about evangelism. The key to this discussion is found in questions 3 and 4: realizing that fears can be overcome and then dreaming together about what could happen.

Homework
Quickly go over the material to be studied by the members before the next session. Urge them to invite friends to join the training group. Provide extra copies of *Small Group Evangelism* that they can pass along to friends who want to join the group so that these friends too can prepare for next week.

Session 2: The Problems in Witnessing

Aims
1. To continue the group-building process by generating discussion around a shared experience; and to incorporate new members into the group.
2. To learn how to invite people to a small group.
3. To help people identify their own problems in personal witnessing, understand how to overcome these and feel hopeful that they can do so.
4. To catch a sense of excitement about outreach by examining the experience of the early church; and then to covenant together to seek to become such a witnessing community.

Pregroup Planning
Anticipate that at least a few new people will join the group. Think about how to make them feel welcome. Be aware of the "tone" or "feeling" you want the group

to have—clear insight into genuine problems but with a hope that these can be overcome coupled with a sense of growing excitement about small group evangelism. Also, identify the logistical problems you had last week and work to overcome these (for instance, problems of space, interruptions and so on).

In case not everyone brings their copy of Scripture, you may want to have extra copies available for the Bible study in the last section of the group session.

Outline
A. The Art of Invitation (30 min.)
B. Witnessing and Me (20 min.)
C. The Witnessing Community (40 min.)
 1. Bible Study
 2. Covenant

A. The Art of Invitation (30 min.)
You have several goals in this discussion. First, help people to understand the *mechanics of invitation:* how do you invite people so that they are likely to respond positively? This exercise looks forward to the time when the group members will be inviting non-Christian friends to the Outreach Event. Sum up the insights that are generated about the process of invitation. Help the group see that people are more likely to respond positively if you communicate enthusiasm, help them overcome hindrances from attending (for example, by providing transportation), are completely honest in the invitation and are sensitive to a genuine no.

The second goal is to help people get in touch with their *feelings* about inviting people to a small group (see, for example, question 5).

The third goal is to discuss what does or does not motivate people. Why did members find it hard (or easy) to get around to inviting people? Why were people reluctant (or eager) to come? If your group has not yet gained any new members, do not let them be discouraged. Try to discover together why no one else came. Learn from this experience. The problem may be that group members simply did not get around to asking anyone—or only did so at the last moment. Do not chide them for this! Instead, use the time to discuss why they didn't get around to asking others. This question of motivation will be picked up in the Bible study.

You need not take the questions in order. Switch back and forth from the inviters to the invited. For example, after asking, "How did you go about inviting people?" turn to those who were invited and ask, "What was it about this small group that interested you?"

C. The Witnessing Community (40 min.)
Question 1. Note the characteristics of that first-century group. They all seemed to be friends; they reported back to one another; they were a praying community; they were persecuted; they expected miracles; they were filled by the Holy Spirit; they

spoke the word of God boldly; they experienced answers to prayer; they saw concrete results; they had real unity. But do not simply give the answers. Allow people the joy and excitement of self-discovery.

Question 2. This touches the whole issue of motivation. This was an exciting, explosive community which experienced great success in evangelism. Why?

Make sure that the group notes the motivating power of "signs and wonders," of the disciples' experience of the Trinity (a trust in the sovereign God, an awareness of the resurrected and hence living Christ and an infilling of the Holy Spirit) and the motivating power of genuine Christian fellowship. Focus your discussion eventually on Acts 4:31, concerning the experience of being filled with the Holy Spirit. Help the group to visualize what happened then. What does it mean to "be filled with the Holy Spirit"?

Question 3. If there is time, move to question 3. How can we in this small group become a warm fellowship in touch with the power of the Triune God?

Move on to the question of the group covenant. Each individual will have thought about his or personal covenant (p. 54). Now prepare a group covenant. The group may simply affirm the covenant on p. 54 or forge their own group covenant. (See *Small Group Leaders' Handbook* published by InterVarsity Press, pp. 141-42 for insight into the covenanting process.)

Homework
Remind people of their homework for the coming week (p. 150). You might want to have available, for purchase or loan, copies of the IVP booklet *Tyranny of the Urgent* by Charles Hummel. Mention also that in a few weeks the small group will be holding an Outreach Event to which they will be able to invite non-Christian friends.

If other Christians want to get into the training course, another group can be set up for them. But it is too late to join the present group. One-quarter of the course is over, and the group is now beginning to develop an identity and cohesion which would be disrupted by the presence of new people.

Session 3: Skills of a Christian Conversationalist

Aims
1. To provide a model of what it means to be a witness, emphasizing honesty, naturalness and good conversational skills.
2. To teach the kind of conversational skills that can be put into practice immediately (sharing honestly, listening carefully and solving problems).
3. To provide experience in using these skills.

Small Group Overview
In this session the group moves into a new phase. Thus far they have been discussing what it means to be a witness. In this session the group will begin to learn the skills that will enable them to witness. The first two sessions were familiar activities— discussion, Bible study and sharing. In the more demanding (and potentially threatening) group activities of session 3, your enthusiasm for the exercises will allay any fears. This session is always a lot of fun and it leaves people feeling that they have learned something of immediate value and use.

Outline
A. The Christian Conversationalist (10 min.)
B. Sharing Exercise (30 min.)
C. The Art of Listening (20 min.)
D. Problem-Solving (30 min.)

A. The Christian Conversationalist (10 min.)
This is a *brief* warm-up exercise. Do not try to go over all the material in chapter 3.

B. Sharing Exercise (30 min.)
Situation 1 will help people clarify their ideas about the group. This is important because at a later date, group members will be inviting others to attend one of the sessions and may then begin to discuss Christianity with others.

The aim of situation 2 is to help people put into words the personal significance of their Christian experience.

Situation 3 concerns witness by means of our actions. Note carefully: do the responses by group members indicate a willingness to get involved with the other person, or is there an attempt to help only in some remote way?

The questions are intended to draw attention to some of the natural opportunities we have to share our faith and, by requiring members to think through and formulate responses, to give people confidence to begin to do so.

You may need to substitute situations more appropriate to your small group. In a university group, for example, the first situation will work, but situation 2 might be: "Your roommate rolls out of the sack just as you return from church. He casts a sleepy eye your way and says, 'I can't believe you get up early on Sunday to go to church. Why do you do it? What do you get out of church?' " Situation 3 might be rephrased: "You hear that one of the women in your psychology class is going to have to return home in the middle of the semester since her father is critically ill." You *act* as a Christian by . . .

C. The Art of Listening (20 min.)
If possible, practice this exercise with a friend prior to session 3 and then demonstrate

it to the group.

D. Problem-Solving (30 min.)

If possible, role play with a volunteer how problem-solving works. You will probably want to set up this role play prior to the group meeting. Pick a familiar problem. For example, "My roommate and I do not get along. What can I do?"

Another option is to do this problem-solving exercise in pairs. Then each person will have more time. Or you might ask the group to critique your demonstration role play and not break up into individual pairs or triads.

Session 4: The Process of Planning

Aims

1. To introduce the idea and experience of group prayer.
2. To teach the process of planning small group outreach.
3. To plan an actual Outreach Event.

Outline

A. Group Prayer (30 min.)
B. Planning an Outreach Event (1 hour)

A. Group Prayer (30 min.)

If conversational prayer is a new idea for the group, then spend the first five minutes introducing it and answering any questions. As leader, you will need to be sensitive to the real fears some people have about praying in public. Conversational prayer makes group prayer easier, but you might want to suggest that people write a brief prayer which they can read if praying in public is new to them. See Rosalind Rinker's *Prayer: Conversing with God* (Zondervan) for more insight.

B. Planning an Outreach Event (1 hour)

This is the exercise in which many people finally grasp that you will really be doing evangelism together. There will be a real excitement (and some fear) as you start planning.

Review the ideas. Review the five aspects of planning, but do not take too much time at this (five minutes or less). You will learn the process by doing it together. Occasionally some groups (because they are afraid of evangelism) will try to divert the planning into a long discussion about this or that point. Do not allow this. Keep the group on track.

Plan the event. Notice that the first question relates to the target group. Unless you know who you are seeking to reach, you cannot plan effectively. Next I suggest that you move to the question of content: what topic will be tackled and how? This is the key question and the one to which you want to give the bulk of your time. The other three questions will probably answer themselves in the course of this content planning.

Resist the temptation to be too elaborate. It is not realistic, for example, to attempt to produce a slide show in order to introduce your topic. Do not pick a topic too broad to be dealt with (for example, "The Problem of Evil"). Be simple. Be focused. Do something you can manage comfortably.

How will evangelism be done during this Outreach Event? Often such one-time events are pre-evangelistic. Your aim might be simply to get people interested enough to come to whatever series you plan at the conclusion of the training course.

Make sure someone is attending to each detail. Summarize at the end who is doing what and when it must be done.

Session 5: The Interactions of a Small Group

Aims
1. To continue praying together about the Outreach Event.
2. To discuss basic group dynamics in such a way as to:
   a. help each person identify how he or she relates in a group,
   b. help the group face problems it may have and
   c. help prepare people for the Outreach Event by giving them confidence that they know how to conduct a group session and handle any problems that might arise.

Outline
A. Group Prayer (15 min.)
B. Group Process (1 hour)
C. Group Planning (15 min.)

A. Group Prayer (15 min.)
Begin with a time of prayer. You may want to split the group into smaller units of three or four people in order to allow more time for individuals to pray. Remind the group to be specific in what they pray and confident that God will work through the Outreach Event.

B. Group Process (1 hour)
In this exercise, aim to help each person to *identify* the role he or she plays in a

small group, to *understand* the value and the potential problem of each role and to *reflect* on how the new understanding of group process will enhance the Outreach Event.

C. Group Planning (15 min.)
Make sure plans for the Outreach Event are going smoothly. You might want to use the suggestions in "Planning an Outreach Event" (pp. 157-58) as a check list to evaluate your planning. *Important:* Get some sense from the group as to how many of their friends will attend.

A Planning Note. It might be a good idea to make session 6 a longer and more relaxed meeting than normal. The group may need to unwind from all the activity and tension involved in setting up and running the Outreach Event. Why not meet half an hour or an hour earlier and have dinner together? If you choose to do this, now (session 5) is the time to make plans.

Session 6: The Content of Our Witness (I)

Aims
1. To learn how to evaluate situations and hence to learn from our experiences.
2. To learn how to cope with our emotional reactions to situations.
3. To begin to learn how to articulate clearly who Jesus is.

Outline
Dinner together (optional)
A. Evaluating the Outreach Event (30 min.)
B. Who Jesus Is (1 hour)

A. Evaluating the Outreach Event (30 min.)
If people have not completed the questionnaire "Evaluating Our Group Outreach," begin by allowing five to seven minutes for everyone to do so. Then work through each of the seven questions. What you want is a good mix of sharing feelings, comparing insights, evaluating results and noting lessons. Question 7 is crucial to your planning for the Outreach Series coming up after the training course ends.

As leader, remain positive and optimistic. Remember: mistakes are not tragedies, they are opportunities for learning. Do not let the group be discouraged if your Outreach Event did not go exactly as planned.

B. Who Jesus Is (1 hour)
Your main job for this exercise will probably be that of timekeeper. Use the first five

minutes for splitting into triads and reading the instructions. Then take fifteen minutes for each of the three dialogs. Use the final ten minutes for group reflection on the process of expressing who Jesus is. An alternative form of this exercise would involve two group members playing the different roles, while the whole group acts as observer and evaluates each aspect of the role play on the basis of the material in chapter 6.

Session 7: The Content of Our Witness (II)

Aims
1. To come to grips with our own experience of Christ and be able to express it to others.
2. To learn how to introduce others to Jesus.

Outline
A. Spiritual Pilgrimage (45 min.)
B. Becoming a Christian (45 min.)

A. Spiritual Pilgrimage (45 min.)
There are two parts to this exercise—the individual work which each person does alone (allow ten to fifteen minutes for this) and the sharing of stories in groups of three.

Distribute paper and pencils and explain the first part of the exercise. Refer to the sample sketch. The purpose of this exercise is not thorough identification of past spiritual experience. Rather, it is to get an overall sense of how God has made himself known to us in the past. This "remembering" refreshes our faith and will encourage group members to share this reality with others. A second purpose is to help people identify and articulate how they came to Christ. Such "personal testimonies" are a valuable part of one's witness, especially in concert with the objective facts about the gospel. Having said, "This is the gospel," we need to add, "and this is how I know it works."

After ten to fifteen minutes, divide the group into threes. Each person has five minutes to share his or her story with the other two.

B. Becoming a Christian (45 min.)
Split into triads again. Do three runs—seven minutes for dialog and five minutes for debriefing for each cycle.

Session 8: The Strategy of Small Group Evangelism

Aims
1. To summarize what was learned in the training course and to discuss the application of these lessons.
2. To initiate the planning of the Outreach Series.
3. To say goodbye in the context of worship and sharing.

Outline
A. Past and Future (30 min.)
B. Outreach Series (30 min.)
C. Worship and Praise (30 min.)

A. Past and Future (30 min.)
Let this be a time of general sharing. You will not be able to cover all fifteen questions, nor should you try. Simply use these as a springboard to reflection on past lessons and dreaming about future plans.

B. Outreach Series (30 min.)
The sharing in section A will lead naturally into planning the Outreach Series. The key decision you must make is how to split your group to make room for new people to join. The nature of the split often depends on who you will seek to reach.

Once this key decision is made, allow the subgroups to gather and decide when and where they will meet in order to begin planning their Outreach Series. With what time remains, they can begin brainstorming about how they will structure the Outreach Series.

C. Worship and Praise (30 min.)
You will probably want to prepare somewhat for this. You might want to bring along song sheets, a guitar, Bibles and other materials for use in worship. Begin this time of worship with a brief prayer and a verse of a hymn, but then let the service unfold as it will. You may need to encourage people to share a word of testimony or thanks. What good things happened to them because they were part of the group?

A Thirteen-Week Plan

If you use *Small Group Evangelism* in your weekly Sunday-school or adult-education class, typically you will have thirteen weeks at your disposal. Below I have outlined how you might use this material within a one-hour time frame spread over thirteen weeks.

Week 1
Small Group Exercises:
1. Leader's Introduction (10 min.)   p. 145
2. Getting to Know One Another (20 min.)   p. 145
3. My Hopes and Fears about Evangelism (30 min.)   p. 146
Homework:
Read chapter 1 and prepare interaction materials
Invite Christian friends to join the class

Week 2
Small Group Exercises:
1. The Art of Invitation (20 min.)   p. 148
2. The Witnessing Community (40 min.)   p. 149
Homework:
Read chapter 2 and prepare interaction materials

Week 3
Small Group Exercises:
1. Discuss chapter 2 (20 min.)
2. Witnessing and Me (40 min.)   p. 149
Homework:
Read chapter 3 and prepare interaction materials

Week 4
Small Group Exercises:
1. The Christian Conversationalist (20 min.)   p. 151

2. Sharing Exercise (40 min.)   p. 151
Homework:
Do "Sharing Our Faith with Others"   p. 62

Week 5
Small Group Exercises:
1. The Art of Listening (25 min.)   p. 152
2. Problem-Solving (35 min.)   p. 153
Homework:
Read chapter 4 and prepare interaction materials

Week 6
Small Group Exercise:
Planning an Outreach Event (1 hour)   p. 157
Homework:
Read chapter 5 and prepare interaction materials

Week 7
Small Group Exercise:
Group Process (1 hour)   p. 159
Homework:
Invite friends to Outreach Event

Week 8
Small Group Exercises:
1. Finish planning Outreach Event (30 min.)
2. Group Prayer (30 min.)   p. 159
Homework:
Prepare for Outreach Event

Week 9
This will be the Outreach Event to which you invite friends and for which you made plans.
Homework:
Read chapter 6 and do "Evaluating Our Group Outreach" in interaction exercises

Week 10
Small Group Exercises:
1. Evaluating the Outreach Event (30 min.)   p. 164
2. Discuss chapter 6 (30 min.)
Homework:
Do "A Dialog about Jesus"   p. 110

Week 11
Small Group Exercise:
Who Jesus Is (1 hour)   p. 164

Homework:
Read chapter 7 and prepare interaction materials

Week 12
Small Group Exercises:
Spiritual Pilgrimage (30 min.)   p. 166
Becoming a Christian (30 min.)   p. 167
Homework:
Read chapter 8 and prepare interaction materials

Week 13
Small Group Exercises:
1. Past and Future (30 min.)   p. 169
2. Worship and Praise (30 min.)   p. 169

Notes

Introduction

[1]John L. Casteel, ed., *Spiritual Renewal through Personal Groups* (New York: Association Press, 1957), p. 17.

1: Understanding Outreach

[1]David B. Barrett, ed., *World Christian Encyclopedia* (Oxford: Oxford University Press, 1982), p. 3. The 1984 World Population Data Sheet estimated the 1983 world population to be 4.76 billion and projected an increase to 6 billion by 2000.

[2]Leighton Ford, *The Christian Persuader* (New York: Harper and Row, 1966), pp. 48-50.

[3]Hans-Ruedi Weber, "The Spontaneous Missionary Church," *Laity* 4 (May 1962):75.

[4]Ibid., p. 72.

[5]Ibid., p. 73.

[6]This theorem is named for Kenneth Strachan, the former director of the Latin America Mission who did much of this research. Much of the information concerning Latin America Mission is taken from *Evangelism-in-Depth: Experimenting with a New Type of Evangelism* (Chicago: Moody Press, 1961). The theorem quoted is found on p. 25. Subsequent analysis of the Evangelism-in-Depth movement has shown that an additional step is necessary for the results of these evangelistic efforts to be conserved: there must be a viable plan for incorporating new believers into churches.

[7]For example, "Plan Rosario," an evangelistic campaign in Rosario, Argentina. See C. Peter Wagner, "Plan Rosario: Milepost for Saturation Evangelism?" *Church Growth Bulletin* 14, no. 1 (September 1977):145-49; and E. Edgardo Silvoso, "In Rosario It Was Different—Crusade Converts Are in the Churches," *Evangelical Missions Quarterly* 14 (April 1978):83-87.

[8]For example, C. Peter Wagner, *Your Spiritual Gifts Can Help Your Church Grow* (Glendale, Calif.: Gospel Light, Regal Books, 1979) and Donald Bridge and David Phypers, *Spiritual Gifts and the Church* (Downers Grove, Ill.: InterVarsity Press,

1973).

[9]Wagner, *Your Spiritual Gifts*, pp. 90-96.

[10]Leighton Ford, *Letters to a New Christian* (Minneapolis: The Billy Graham Evangelistic Association, 1967), p. 43.

[11]Ibid., pp. 43-44.

[12]Richard Peace, *A Church's Guide to Evangelism* (Boston: The Evangelistic Association of New England, 1982), pp. 12-13.

2: Overcoming Doubts and Fears

[1]Paul Little, "What Non-Christians Ask," *HIS* 21 (November 1960):1.

[2]Bishop John Carter, *Methods of Mission in Southern Africa* (London: S.P.C.K., 1963), p. 99.

[3]John White, "Witnessing Is Not Brainwashing," *HIS* 26 (June 1966):6.

[4]D. T. Niles, *That They May Have Life* (New York: Harper and Row, 1961), p. 96.

3: Communicating Our Faith

[1]John White, "Witnessing is Not Brainwashing," pp. 5-6.

[2]Bruce Larson, *Setting Men Free* (Grand Rapids, Mich.: Zondervan, 1967), pp. 27-28.

[3]For many of us, lack of honesty is a defense mechanism against hurt buried deep in our past. In this case, honesty may require the help of a counselor or therapist.

[4]William Barclay, *The Gospel of Mark* (Edinburgh: The Saint Andrew Press, 1957), p. 116.

[5]Adapted from *Learning to Love People* by Richard Peace (Grand Rapids, Mich.: Zondervan, 1968), pp. 24-30.

4: Designing Small Group Outreach

[1]Note in Mark 2:14-17, that Matthew (here called Levi) begins his discipleship with Jesus by inviting his friends and colleagues into his home to meet Jesus. Throughout the New Testament, homes are used constantly for worship, prayer, counseling and evangelism.

[2]Samuel Shoemaker, *The Experiment of Faith* (New York: Harper and Row, 1957), p. 14.

[3]Abraham Maslow asserts that all human beings have the same set of needs and furthermore these needs are arranged in an order of priority: (1) Physical needs: food, water, warmth, sleep and so on; (2) security needs: having a place where we feel safe; (3) belonging needs: the need to love and be loved; (4) esteem needs: being accepted as playing a special role in one's community; (5) self-actualization needs: that which comes out of aesthetic pursuits, creativity, intellectual fulfillment, mystical experience, and so on. Maslow further asserts that, until a lower level need is met, a person will not be concerned about other needs. A starving person is not able to be interested in pursuing creative endeavors. Maslow

feels that most Americans function at level three. They are engaged in a frantic quest for love and acceptance—which accords with my assertion that the kind of fellowship one finds in a small group is greatly desired by people in general. See Keith Miller, *The Becomers* (Waco, Tex.: Word, 1973), chapters 12 and 13 for further information about Maslow's hierarchy of needs and the implications of this model for evangelism.

[4]Weber, "The Spontaneous Missionary Church," pp. 74-75.

[5]Michael Green has an illuminating section on the value of small groups in his book *Evangelism in the Early Church* (Grand Rapids, Mich.: Eerdmans, 1970) pp. 207-8: "One of the most important methods of spreading the Gospel in antiquity was by the use of homes. It had positive advantages: the comparatively small numbers involved made real interchange of views and informal discussion among the participants possible; there was no artificial isolation of a preacher from his hearers; . . . the sheer informality and relaxed atmosphere of the home, not to mention the hospitality which must often have gone with it, all helped to make this form of evangelism particularly successful. . . . Household evangelism is a significant feature in the New Testament itself. Jason's house at Thessalonica was used for this purpose (Acts 17:5), so was that of Titius Justus, situated provocatively opposite the synagogue (with which Paul had broken) at Corinth (Acts 18:7). Philip's house at Caesarea seems to have been a most hospitable place where not only visiting seafarers like Paul and his company but wandering charismatics like Agabus were made welcome (Acts 21:10-11). Both Lydia's house and the jailer's at Philippi were used as evangelistic centers (Acts 16:15, 32-4), and Stephanas apparently used his home at Corinth in the same way (1 Cor 1:16 and 16:15). . . . The very earliest Christian community met in the upper room of a particular house, owned by the mother of John Mark in Jerusalem (Acts 1:13 f., 12:12). It is hardly surprising that the 'church in the house' became a crucial factor in the spread of the Christian faith."

[6]Ford, *The Christian Persuader,* pp. 71-72.

[7]However, "Let your love be genuine" (Rom 12:9). Your motivation cannot be to seek friendships *in order to witness.* You love others because this is what Christianity is all about. Of course, part of love is openness about Christ.

[8]See Em Griffin, *The Mind Changers* (Wheaton, Ill.: Tyndale House, 1976), pp. 57-60 for a fascinating account of his research on crowding.

5: Understanding Group Dynamics

[1]George and Florence Pert, *Get Going through Small Groups* (Carmel, N.Y.: Guideposts Associates, 1969), p. 19.

[2]Clyde Reid, *Groups Alive—Church Alive* (New York: Harper and Row, 1969), p. 47.

[3]Ibid., p. 48.

[4]Dietrich Bonhoeffer, *Life Together* (New York: Harper and Row, 1949), p. 86.

[5]D. T. Niles, *That They May Have Life* (New York: Harper and Row, 1961), p. 96.

[6]Samuel Shoemaker, quoted in Pert, *Get Going through Small Groups,* p. 17.
[7]Bruce Larson, "A New Breed of Men," in *Groups in Action,* ed. Lyman Coleman (Newtown, Pa.: Halfway House, 1968), p. 56.
[8]I am not suggesting, however, that you walk into a group and "hang up all your dirty linen in public." That's exhibitionism, not honesty. The nature of the group will define the bounds of sharing. The key thing, though, is no pretense.
[9]Paul Miller, *Group Dynamics in Evangelism* (Scottdale, Pa.: Herald Press, 1958), p. 93.

6: Talking about Jesus

[1]C. S. Lewis, "What Are We to Make of Jesus Christ?" *Asking Them Questions,* quoted in Clyde S. Kilby, ed., *A Mind Awake* (New York: Harper and Row, 1968), p. 92.
[2]C. S. Lewis, *Mere Christianity* (New York: Macmillan, 1974), pp. 52-53.
[3]Ibid., pp. 54-55.
[4]Em Griffin, *The Mind Changers,* p. 93.

7: Introducing Others to Jesus

[1]Mary McDermott Shideler, *A Creed for a Christian Skeptic* (Grand Rapids, Mich.· Eerdmans, 1968), p. 98.
[2]Lyman Coleman, *Encyclopedia of Serendipity* (Littleton, Colo.: Serendipity House, 1976, 1980), p. 87. Coleman includes twelve other affirmation exercises in this book. See his many books for both the theory of affirmation and a host of practical small group exercises by which to express it.
[3]See, for example, "The Missing Piece—A Case Study" in Richard Peace, *Giving Your Faith and Keeping It Too* (Elgin, Ill.: David C. Cook, 1979) in the Christian Growth Elective series.
[4]Burton Harding, "What Is the Gospel?" *HIS* 26 (February 1966):6.
[5]Ibid.
[6]Shideler, *A Creed for a Christian Skeptic,* p. 95.
[7]Ibid., pp. 36-37.
[8]See Richard Peace, *Pilgrimage* (Grand Rapids, Mich.: Baker, 1984), chapter 8, for a discussion of how repentance and faith are the key to growth in the Christian life.
[9]Paul Little, *How to Give Away Your Faith* (Downers Grove, Ill.: InterVarsity Press, 1966), p. 69.
[10]John R. W. Stott, *Basic Christianity* (Downers Grove, Ill.: InterVarsity Press, 1958), p. 131. You may well ask how such an act of commitment relates to infant baptism and confirmation. In baptism, vows are made on behalf of the infant by the parents. Furthermore, the parents vow to raise the child in the Christian faith, so that at confirmation a child is ready to co-affirm these vows, to confirm as an adult the intention to follow Christ.

8: Planning for the Future
[1]Weber, "The Spontaneous Missionary Church," p. 75.
[2]Douglas Hyde, *Dedication and Leadership: Learning from Commitment* (Notre Dame, Ind.: Notre Dame University Press, 1966), p. 93.

Part 2: The Experience
[1]This exercise was suggested by A. J. T. Cook, "Handbook of Lay-Involvement" (Johannesburg, South Africa, n.d.), p. 26.
[2]C. S. Lewis, *Christian Reflections* (Grand Rapids, Mich.: Eerdmans, 1967), p. 33.